IT'S GETTING

HOT

IN HERE

For Cynthia Platt, editor extraordinaire

Copyright © 2015 by Bridget Heos

For information about permission to reproduce selections from this
book, write to Permissions, Houghton Mifflin Harcourt
Publishing Company, 215 Park Avenue South,
New York, New York 10003.

www.hmhco.com

Library of Congress Cataloging-in-Publication Data is available

ISBN 978-0-544-30347-8

Printed in Malaysia

TWP 10 9 8 7 6 5 4 3 2 1

4500553935

Jacket photos: cracked earth, raincoat, swirling clouds, flooded houses, and palm tree
© Corbis; iceberg © Mark Karrass/Corbis; salty earth landscape © Gary Weathers/
Getty Images; oil drilling © H. David Seawell/Corbis; children © Ozan Köse/iStock;
electric car © Simon Turner/Alamy; solar panels © Elenathewise/Fotolia; desert land
© one AND only/Shutterstock; polar bear and burned paper © Veer; stop sign © Getty.

IT'S GETTING HOT IN HERE

The Past, Present, and Future of
Climate Change

BRIDGET HEOS

HOUGHTON MIFFLIN HARCOURT
Boston New York

CONTENTS

1   Introduction

11   PART ONE: SUCH A PERFECT WORLD

12   Chapter 1: The Greenhouse Effect

19   Chapter 2: How Climate Works

28   PART TWO: TO UNDERSTAND THE FUTURE,

     WE HAVE TO GO BACK IN TIME

30   Chapter 3: It All Started with a Big Bang

46   Chapter 4: Rise of the Planet of the Humans

56   Chapter 5: Humans + Fossil Fuels: A Love Story

65   PART THREE: IS IT HOT IN HERE, OR IS IT JUST ME?

     HOW WE KNOW THE EARTH IS WARMING

66   Chapter 6: The Discovery of Global Warming

74   Chapter 7: The Evidence Today

95   Chapter 8: But How Do We Know That *We're* Causing Global Warming?

101   Chapter 9: How Are We Causing Global Warming?

122   PART FOUR: NATURE AND HUMAN NATURE

124   Chapter 10: Nature's Fury: How Hot? How Bad?

138   Chapter 11: So Should I Be Worried?

148   Chapter 12: The Politics of Global Warming

156   Chapter 13: A Little Less Talk, a Lot More Action

171   PART FIVE: LET'S DO THIS!

172   Chapter 14: Be Efficient. B. E. Efficient

186   Chapter 15: With Great Power Comes Great Responsibility

196   Glossary
201   For Further Reading
202   Notes
204   Select Bibliography
218   Photo Credits
221   Index

INTRODUCTION

Kiribati, a nation of thirty-three islands in the middle of the Pacific Ocean, is home to 103,000 people. And it is drowning. Flooding has always occurred during storms. But now, the floodwater never recedes and villages are left permanently flooded. Meanwhile, ocean water has polluted the fresh groundwater, making it undrinkable. Scientists say that by the end of this century, the entire nation will have been swallowed by the sea because of global warming. The people, known as the I-Kiribati, will be among the first global warming refugees.

In the Pacific island nation of Kiribati, tree roots are exposed due to erosion that happens during high tides. Rising sea level is causing Kiribati to slowly be swallowed by the sea.

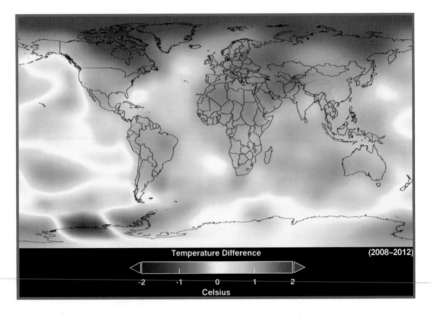

Temperature Difference (2008–2012)

-2 -1 0 1 2
Celsius

The temperature is rising almost worldwide, as seen on this map. Global warming is occurring most rapidly in the Arctic, resulting in melting glaciers and, as a result, rising sea level.

The world is getting warmer. The global temperature has risen 1.4 degrees F (0.85 degrees C) since 1880. If you're reading this on a cold day, you might think, "Why is warmer bad?" Well, it isn't, always. Warm or cold, there's no such thing as a perfect world. The dinosaurs survived in a warmer world. Mammoths and other megafauna thrived in a colder one. But Earth, with its present climate, is *our* perfect world because it's the world to which we as humans have adapted and thrived. Our population has swelled in this perfect world, our nations' borders were drawn according to it, and our food and water supplies depend upon it.

The earth's climate has changed through the years. But we humans have come to rely on the present climate to grow food, access fresh water, and avoid flooding. As such, it is our "perfect world," but global warming is changing that.

As the earth warms, it disrupts our perfect world in many ways. Kiribati is just one of many island nations being inundated by the rising sea, and the people of these nations can't simply move to higher ground. That land already belongs to other countries, the governments of which are reluctant to take in refugees because it would require an investment of time and money. In the case of Kiribati, the government has purchased land in nearby Fiji for the purpose of relocating. But Fiji is opposed to the idea of taking in a whole nation of people. Even when entire countries aren't wiped out, coastal cities will be inundated by the rising tides. The cities' infrastructures will be damaged by every major storm, until it no longer makes sense to rebuild. Citizens of these cities will also need to find new homes.

Even as flooding becomes commonplace, water shortages will abound. As is the case in the Pacific islands, coastal water supplies will be polluted by salt water. Elsewhere, water supplies will dry up because of droughts and shrinking glaciers. This will eventually lead to a decrease in food supply, as plants need water to grow. If global warming is left unchecked, our perfect world will become a world of heartbreaking struggle. In places where flooding and drought have taken hold, the struggle is already under way.

The less we allow the earth to warm, the fewer problems we will have. And every degree counts. Because when it comes to global temperature, small changes make a big difference. During the last ice age (which occurred from 2.5 million to 10,000 years ago), mile-deep glaciers overtook much of the Northern Hemisphere. And the world was just 9 degrees F (5 degrees C) colder on average than it is now. Today, with less than 1.4 degrees F (0.85 degree C) of warming, trouble is afoot. Sea level has risen 7.5 inches (19 centimeters), which is why island nations are slowly drowning. Global warming has also brought about droughts, heat waves, wildfires, and storms, and led to the spread of tropical diseases and the extinction of species. The evidence is clear: global warming is real and is already causing suffering.

It's also clear that global warming is the result of rising

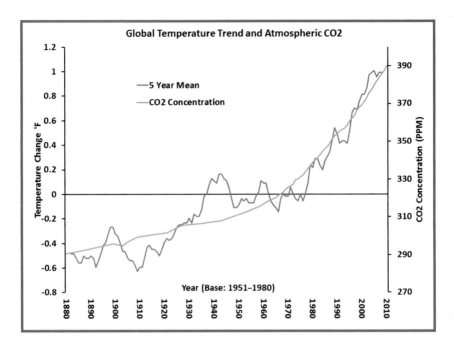

Global Temperature Trend and Atmospheric CO2

Carbon dioxide levels (the green line) and the global temperature (the blue line) have risen together since 1880. This is a key piece of evidence that shows that increased greenhouse gases in the atmosphere are causing global warming.

greenhouse gas emissions caused by human activity. Carbon dioxide in the atmosphere is measured in parts per million. This means that for every million molecules of gas in the atmosphere, there are a certain number of carbon dioxide molecules contained therein. For instance, 400 parts per million is equivalent to four hundred molecules of carbon dioxide per million total molecules of gas. From the end of the last ice age, ten thousand years ago, to the beginning of the Industrial Revolution in 1760, carbon dioxide levels in the atmosphere hovered around 280 parts per million. But as coal began to power industry and electricity, and oil came to power our vehicles, greenhouse gas levels rose. Deforestation and modern agriculture practices have added to this effect. As a result, carbon dioxide levels are now nearing 400 parts per million—41 percent higher than pre–Industrial Revolution levels.

Today, scientists are studying global warming so that we can prepare for its future effects and stop it from getting out of hand. Many leaders are taking heed, hoping to prevent the human suffering and costly damage that will occur as the temperature climbs higher. Military, government, business, and community leaders are curbing emissions by increasing efficiency, switching to renewable energy, and changing forestry and agricultural practices. But there is still much to be done. If we are to stop the global temperature from rising more than 3.6 degrees F (2 degrees C)—the current international goal—then developed and developing nations will need to reduce their greenhouse gas emissions significantly. In 1990, the carbon dioxide level was a little over 350 parts per million. According to scientists, 350 parts per million is the level to which we need to return in order to avoid some of the most devastating effects of global warming. The Intergovernmental Panel on Climate Change (IPCC), a United Nations group of climate scientists, recommends that nations turn back time on their emissions so that they become lower than they were in 1990.

In America, uniting to achieve that goal may be difficult, as some political leaders are acting on the view that global warming doesn't exist, that humans are not causing it, or that it is not a concern. Because this book is rooted in science, it will not explore this viewpoint, which is a political and not a scientific one. Scientists agree that human-induced global warming is well under way, and that it is cause for great concern.

This book will first take a look at climate and the history of climate change. Then it will show the evidence that global warming is already happening and describe how we as humans are causing it. Next, it will address the role human psychology and politics play in global warming. Finally, it will present the path toward lowering greenhouse gas emissions and rescuing the world from dangerous warming. I hope that this book will be a call to action. Being informed and making small changes today can lead to bigger changes as you enter the workforce, step into leadership roles, and build a life. Global warming is already happening, but that doesn't mean it's too late to act. It's always the right time to do the right thing.

BE THE CHANGE

Mahatma Gandhi said, "If we could change ourselves, the tendencies in the world would also change." This has been popularly revised into the slogan "Be the change you wish to see in the world." In each chapter, you'll be given one or more suggestions to "be the change" that combats global warming.

That's not to say that if you did all of these things, the problem of global warming would be solved. Saying "If only people would compost, we wouldn't have all these glaciers melting!" would be akin to saying that if only people would be nice to their neighbors, all wars would end. Sure, every little bit helps, but isn't it up to our leaders to bring about real change?

The thing is, our leaders are people just like us, and some of us are already leaders in our schools and neighborhoods. If we make small changes at home and in our communities, they may lead to changes on a larger scale. For instance, if you save energy at home by turning off lights, adjusting the heat and air conditioning, and powering down computers, you might later lead the charge to bring a wind turbine to your school. Then you may become a state official who brings wind energy to your entire state. As you can see, if everyone made these changes, it really would make a difference. After all, change doesn't happen all at once, but starts small and grows.

The changes suggested here cost nothing or even save money. The reason for this is twofold. First, most families don't have extra money to spend on new projects. Second, environmental decisions will always come up against money considerations, and luckily, conserving energy really is a great way to save money. It's good to start thinking that way now. So go ahead. Get out there and be the change.

PART ONE
SUCH A PERFECT WORLD

CHAPTER 1
THE GREENHOUSE EFFECT

PEOPLE OFTEN SAY THAT IN a perfect world, this would happen or that would happen. In a perfect world, grades would be based on effort alone. In a perfect world, nice guys would always finish first. In a perfect world, cupcakes would grow on trees and therefore be fruit and therefore be health food, and so on. But our world already *is* pretty perfect. It has to be in order for life to exist. Even simple life forms have yet to be found on other planets. But here on earth, conditions have allowed complex plants and animals to evolve. For humans to have populated the world and built civilizations that provide food, water, health care, and education, things needed to be *just right*. To be sure, disaster, injustice, and tragedy create dire circumstances, but by and large, you and I owe our existence to the perfect world we live in.

One of the most important factors in our world is the greenhouse effect. Without it, Earth would be too cold to support life. Earth's average temperature is 59 degrees F (15 degrees C), but without the greenhouse effect, it would be

0 degrees F (–18 degrees C)—in other words, we would be a ball of ice. Other planets also have greenhouse effects. Without it, Venus, which averages a toasty 855 degrees F (457 degrees C), would plunge to –63 degrees F (–53 degrees C). The difference is so drastic because of its thick greenhouse gases. Nicknamed Earth's evil twin because of its similar size and composition but scorching heat, Venus may have been more Earth-like a billion years ago. For instance, it may have had oceans. Scientists theorize that because Venus is closer than Earth to the sun, any oceans Venus may have had would have evaporated due to the greater heat that proximity brings. The water would have become water vapor, a heat-trapping gas that would have caused the planet's temperature to rise

The greenhouse effect is so strong on Venus that its average temperature is 855 degrees F (457 degrees C), compared to Earth's 59 degrees F (15 degrees C). Venus is similar to Earth in some ways, and for this reason the blazing hot planet is sometimes called Earth's evil twin.

higher. This would have accelerated the evaporation until Venus had no water left at all. Without oceans or a water cycle, carbon dioxide would have remained in the atmosphere rather than being absorbed by the water. This too would have trapped heat, causing the temperature to soar. Today, Venus's surface could melt lead. (As dangerous as global warming is, rest assured that most scientists do not think it will cause Earth to become like Venus.)

So what exactly *is* the greenhouse effect? It's a process that occurs in a planet's atmosphere (the layer of air that extends from the surface to outer space). The earth's atmosphere is made up of gases, mainly nitrogen and oxygen, but also greenhouse gases: carbon dioxide, methane, water vapor, and a few others. These gases trap heat. How exactly do they do this? The sun's energy enters the atmosphere as visible radiation, or light. Some of this light is reflected back into space by clouds and particles in the earth's atmosphere and by the earth's surface. But about half of the sun's rays are absorbed by the earth's surface. They become a different kind of radiation: infrared radiation, or heat. This is what warms the surface of the earth and the air close to the surface. Light has no trouble passing through greenhouse gases. But heat does. Greenhouse gases trap some of the heat, keeping the earth warm enough to support life.

Over billions of years, greenhouse gases have allowed life on Earth to flourish. The problem today is that people are rapidly releasing additional greenhouse gases into the

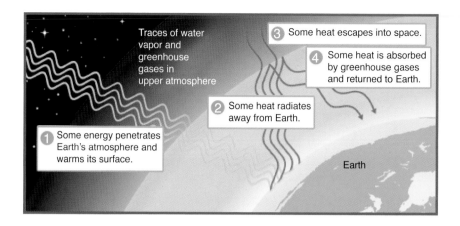

The greenhouse effect is the process by which a planet's atmosphere traps heat from the sun, warming the planet.

atmosphere, and more and more heat is getting trapped. Think of two blankets that cover the same area. One is made with a pound of wool; the other with two pounds of wool. Which would keep you warmer? The heavier one would, of course. In the same way, higher concentrations of greenhouse gases such as carbon dioxide act like an atmospheric blanket to make the earth warmer.

Carbon dioxide is the most talked-about greenhouse gas because it's the most prevalent gas that is emitted by humans—mainly through the burning of coal, oil, and natural gas (collectively known as fossil fuels). Why does burning fossil fuels emit carbon dioxide? Let's look at how these fuels are created: All living things on Earth contain carbon, which is one of the most abundant elements in the universe. When carbon combines with oxygen in the atmosphere, it forms carbon dioxide. One carbon atom combines with two oxygen

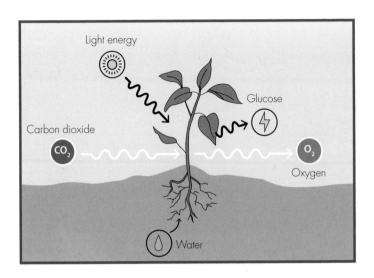

Photosynthesis is the process by which plants convert sunlight, water, and carbon dioxide to plant food (glucose) and oxygen. In this way, plants remove carbon dioxide from the atmosphere.

atoms to form a carbon dioxide molecule. This is why the symbol for carbon dioxide is CO_2.

Plants absorb carbon dioxide from the air. Using chlorophyll and energy from the sun, plants convert carbon and water into glucose, which is a sugar, and oxygen. Glucose is the primary ingredient in plant fibers, so it makes up the plants themselves. The oxygen is emitted into the air. The equation looks like this: CO_2 (carbon dioxide) + H_2O (water) + sunlight = $C_6H_{12}O_6$ (glucose) + O_2 (oxygen). As you can see, the carbon atoms help to make up the glucose molecules. So the carbon is now part of the plants. When the plants die, they may rot or burn, which would release the stored carbon atoms. These then combine with oxygen in the air to form carbon dioxide. This is why deforestation causes greenhouse gas emissions—dead trees equal more carbon dioxide released into the atmosphere as well as fewer trees to store the carbon.

But plants may also become buried underground, where the carbon is preserved. Over millions of years, buried plants can become coal. First, bacteria eat the plants but leave behind carbon- and hydrogen-rich matter. As time passes, this matter is pushed underground through sedimentation and other earth processes. The heat underground further breaks down what's left until it becomes coal, which is composed mainly of carbon. When coal is burned, the carbon that's emitted combines with oxygen in the air to form carbon dioxide.

In the ocean, phytoplankton (microscopic plants) absorb carbon dioxide near the surface, and then die and decay, sinking to the ocean floor, where some get buried. After millions of years, buried plankton can become oil in a process similar to the formation of coal. Both coal and oil are high in carbon because they are made from the remains of plants that stored high levels of carbon. When burned, these fossil fuels release carbon dioxide into the atmosphere that is created from the carbon that nature swept under the rug millions of years ago.

Carbon dioxide isn't the only greenhouse gas we're adding to the atmosphere, of course. Others include methane, nitrous oxide, and fluorinated gases. Released by humans into the atmosphere, these gases are all causing the earth to warm quickly, disrupting the climate on which we have come to rely for our health and well-being. And that's why global warming is so dangerous.

BE THE CHANGE

WHAT: Assess your energy use.

HOW: For one day, keep track of your energy use. Each time you use electricity or fuel, write it down, and include the timespan. For instance, if you charge your phone, write down for how long you charge it. If you turn on a light, write down for how long you leave the light on. If you drive to school (or catch a ride), write down how long the trip is.

At the end of the day, circle any instances where you could have saved energy. Could you have unplugged your phone sooner (after it was fully charged)? Could you have walked to school?

WHY: This will show you easy changes that can conserve energy.

WHAT ELSE: Check your carbon footprint. Your carbon footprint is the amount of carbon dioxide you personally release. You can estimate your carbon footprint and compare it to the average U.S. carbon footprint at www.nature.org/greenliving /carboncalculator/index.htm.

CHAPTER 2
HOW CLIMATE WORKS

GLOBAL WARMING IS ALSO CALLED climate change because, with the warming, other climate factors, such as precipitation, humidity, wind, and seasons, are also changing. But what exactly drives climate?

First, it's important to understand that climate is different from weather. Weather is the atmospheric state (everything happening in the air) in a given place over a short period of time. Climate is the weather in a given place over a long period of time. Weather can't be predicted more than a few days in the future, but climate can. For instance, I live in Kansas City. I can't forecast rain for next July 4. But I can guarantee you it will be a hot July. Hot summers are characteristic of our midwestern climate. Climate can be talked about in terms of a specific place or in terms of the world. And climate *can* be predicted through historic records and computer models.

Several factors determine the different climates from pole to pole. One of the biggest factors is the sun. To observe the sun's effect on climate, consider the Amazon rainforest in

At different times of the year, the sun's rays are directed at the equator, Tropic of Capricorn, or Tropic of Cancer. Because the equator isn't far from the Tropic of Capricorn or Tropic of Cancer, it always gets a lot of sunlight, and so land and water located along the equator is always warm.

South America. Its daytime temperature hovers around 80 degrees F (27 degrees C) year-round. This warmth is due to the fact that the rainforest is situated on the equator. The sun hits the equator directly during much of the year so that the sun's rays are focused on the relatively small area near the equator. At the same time, the sun's rays hit the rest of the earth at a slant, so that the rays are spread out over a larger area. The small area is heated more thoroughly than the larger area. (This is similar to the effect of a space heater heating up a small room but barely warming the rest of the home.)

Of course, the Amazon's 80-degree-F days are not exactly record-breaking high temperatures. The shade from the trees and frequent rainfall stop the temperature from rising higher.

Death Valley in California, on the other hand, set a world-record high of 134 degrees F (57 degrees C) on July 10, 1913. Death Valley isn't near the equator, so why is it so hot? Well, it's close to the Tropic of Cancer, and in June, July, and August, the sun hits the Tropic of Cancer directly. This creates summer in the Northern Hemisphere and causes temperatures in Death Valley to soar. Death Valley is extra hot because it's in the desert, where neither shade nor precipitation cools things down. It's also in a valley, which traps heat.

When the sun directly hits the Tropic of Cancer, the temperature in nearby Death Valley soars. Its extreme summer highs — which can reach above 130 degrees F (54 degrees C) — are also due to the fact that Death Valley is part of a valley that traps heat and a desert that offers little shade or precipitation to cool things down.

The Amazon River winds its way through the Amazon rainforest, where the temperature remains around 80 degrees F (27 degrees C) year-round because of its proximity to the equator.

In the Southern Hemisphere, the sun hits the Tropic of Capricorn at a right angle in December, January, and February, which is why many Australians celebrate Christmas at the beach. But whether the sun directly hits the Tropic of Cancer or the Tropic of Capricorn, the equator is not far away, so the Amazon rainforest is always warm.

The sun isn't the only factor that determines temperature, though. Wind carries warm air to cold places, and cold air to warm places. To see how this works, compare the average winter temperatures in Boston, Massachusetts, and La

Coruna, Spain. The two cities are about the same distance from the equator, and yet, in Boston, the average low in January is a frigid 22.1 degrees F (-5.5 degrees C), whereas in La Coruna, it doesn't even approach freezing but dips to an only slightly chilly 44.6 degrees F (7 degrees C). What gives? In the Northern Hemisphere, wind blows from west to east. So the wind in La Coruna blows in from the Atlantic Ocean, whereas the wind in Boston blows in from the land to the west. That's important because water warms and cools more slowly than land. This is especially true for large bodies of water like oceans. (To test this, go swimming in the coastal waters of Boston in late May, and then again in late August; in that time, the water temperature rises from 58 degrees F [14.4 degrees C] to 68 degrees F [20 degrees C].)

Because the ocean stays cold long into the summer, and warm well into the winter, La Coruna enjoys warm ocean breezes throughout the winter. Boston has no such luck. The surface of land does not retain heat or cold very well. (It does not take an asphalt parking lot long to warm up in the summer, for instance.) So wind coming into Boston from the west is cold all winter long. Farther inland, wind from any direction is coming from land, not sea. These regions also have hot summers and cold winters. This explains the hot July that I can be sure of here in Kansas City.

The oceans also help regulate the temperature worldwide by storing one-quarter to one-half of the carbon dioxide burned as fossil fuels so that it is not released into the atmosphere. Unfortunately, what's good for the atmosphere is bad for the ocean. Carbon combines with water to form carbonic acid. This is a weak acid (it's the same stuff that makes our soda pop bubbly). However, in high concentrations, it is corrosive to shells and corals. Even in lower concentrations, it slows their growth. Mollusks and corals need calcium ions and carbonate ions to grow. Carbonic acid reacts with carbonate ions so that they are no longer available to mollusks and corals for shell and coral building. This interrupts food chains and affects all of the life in and around the ocean—including us.

Climate describes not only temperature but also precipitation. Ninety percent of moisture in the atmosphere comes from the evaporation of the ocean and other bodies of water. Inland regions, away from large bodies of water that evaporate and fall as precipitation, tend to be drier. This is why—millions of years ago—when one giant continent, Pangaea, formed, the climate became drier, favoring reptiles over amphibians. Dry regions can also form because of mountains that block winds and thus the precipitation that winds carry. If you drive through Colorado on Interstate 70, you may see this firsthand. The Eisenhower-Johnson Memorial Tunnel cuts through the Continental Divide (the line along the peaks of the Rocky Mountains that divides rivers flowing to the east and rivers flowing to the west). The mountain range blocks winds from the west that carry precipitation from the Pacific Ocean. This precipitation falls as snow upon the western slope of the mountains. So you can enter the tunnel from the east under clear skies, and exit to the west into a snowstorm.

Subtropical zones — 10 to 40 degrees north or south of the equator — also tend to be dry. Observe a map of the world and you'll see that the deserts of the American Southwest (including Death Valley), the Sahara, the Arabian Desert, and other drylands lie in this zone. Along the equator, on the other hand, are the world's great rainforests, including the

Dry conditions in the American Southwest.

Amazon. This is because winds from the Northern Hemisphere and Southern Hemisphere converge at the equator, carrying precipitation from the north and south. But that same precipitation is carried away from the deserts.

Plants can also contribute to precipitation in a process known as transpiration. Plants absorb water through their roots. This water travels through veins in the plant (which are easily visible; they make up the structure of leaves, for instance). Some of this water seeps through tiny pores on the underside of leaves and evaporates. An estimated 10 percent of water vapor in the atmosphere is released by transpiration. In extremely lush areas like the Amazon, plants can produce half the rainfall. For this reason, deforestation, in addition to contributing to global warming, can change the climate of a region from rainy to dry.

So what does all this have to do with global warming? With climate change, the world's climates are becoming more extreme. Dry regions are becoming drier, leading to droughts throughout the world, and a longer wildfire season in the American Southwest. Wet regions are becoming wetter, causing flooding in countries ranging from Ireland to China. Nearly everywhere is becoming warmer. Our once-perfect climate is changing.

BE THE CHANGE

WHAT: Reduce household emissions.

HOW: Suggest that your family raise the thermostat by one degree in the summer and lower it by one degree in the winter.

WHY: Both heating and cooling contribute to greenhouse gas emissions. Air conditioning is powered by electricity, most of which comes from burning fossil fuels. For that reason, electricity causes 38 percent of U.S. carbon dioxide emissions. Heat is derived from either electricity or fossil fuels such as natural gas, heating oil, and propane. Reduce your heating and cooling use, and you'll reduce your greenhouse gas emissions—and save money.

WHAT ELSE: In the summer, close shades on hot days to keep the house cool. In the winter, open shades to let in heat from the sun. It sounds so simple, yet it can make a big impact.

PART TWO
TO UNDERSTAND THE FUTURE, WE HAVE TO GO BACK IN TIME

CHAPTER 3
IT ALL STARTED
WITH A BIG BANG

How DID WE ARRIVE AT this perfect moment in time, when humans have populated every continent except Antarctica and developed the technology that allows so many to live long, healthy, and comfortable lives? Let's start at the beginning and examine how the climate has changed through the years.

If you've been paying attention in science class, or are a fan of sitcoms, you know that it all started with a Big Bang. About 13.7 billion years ago, the universe was a hot, dense point. That is, though it contained matter, it did not take up space. Then it suddenly expanded, in what is known as the Big Bang, and continues to do so today. As the universe expanded, the matter spread out: But some of the matter clustered together, forming the stars and planets of the earliest galaxies. Later, a cloud of dust known as a nebula gave birth to our solar system. The dust in the nebula was pulled from all directions into the center of the cloud by gravity. The cen-

A nebula such as the Orion Nebula shown here gave birth to our solar system 4.6 billion years ago.

ter of the cloud became denser and hotter until it was the sun. The remaining dust swirling around the sun clumped together, just as specks of dust in your house clump together to become dust bunnies. These clumps became the planets. As a result, Earth formed 4.567 billion years ago. Sixty million years later, an object about the size of Mars crashed into Earth. Pieces from the collision formed the moon. The collision also created the earth's spin and tilt.

Early Earth was uninhabitable. Its surface was a magma ocean and its atmosphere, silicate vapor. (Silicates are the minerals that today make up the earth's crust.) Over the years, the magma cooled to form a solid shell. But without

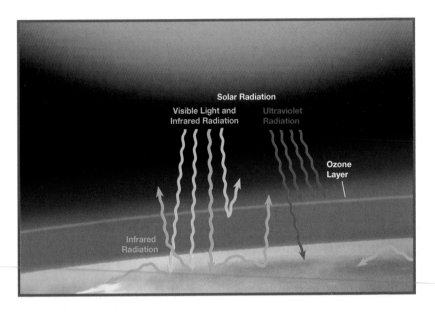

The atmosphere's ozone layer absorbs UV rays, which are harmful to living things. Before the ozone layer developed, it was impossible for complex organisms to evolve.

the protective atmosphere it has today, the planet had no buffer against outer space. It was pounded by meteors, comets, asteroids, and solar winds. Needless to say, this was no place to start a life, even for the toughest bacteria.

Then things started looking up for planet Earth. Liquid metals in the earth's core created a magnetic field around the planet, blocking solar winds. Scientists aren't sure how Earth's first organisms came about, but they theorize that chemicals on Earth at the time formed DNA sequences (which are the instructions that living things use to build and operate themselves) and amino acids (which make up the proteins that are the building blocks of living things). These elements somehow came together to form the first single-celled bacteria.

Early bacteria existed without oxygen. This absence of oxygen also meant that there was no ozone. The ozone, a layer in the atmosphere that is made up of oxygen, absorbs UV rays, protecting the earth from their harmful effects. Even with ozone, some rays still get through, which is why we wear sunscreen today. But with no ozone at all, so many UV rays reached the earth that it was impossible for complex organisms to evolve.

At this time, the earth was warmer than it is now, probably because the atmosphere consisted mainly of nitrogen, methane, carbon dioxide, and ammonia, greenhouse gases that together trap more heat than our atmosphere does today. The oceans could have reached 185 degrees F (85 degrees C). Then the atmosphere suddenly changed. What happened? Oxygen!

If you could travel back in time three billion years, you would see a gray earth. With no oxygen, rocks had not rusted to create the colors brown and red. And the land was mostly barren, so the greenery we see today was nonexistent. Then, 2.4 billion years ago, some of the bacteria in the ocean began to use photosynthesis. Previously, bacteria had been absorbing heat rather than visible light, processing it with a chemical other than chlorophyll, and releasing sulfur instead of oxygen. Some bacteria then began photosynthesizing in the manner we're familiar with today: by absorbing light and releasing oxygen. Oxygen was poisonous to the bacteria living at the time. These organisms survived only if they were buried deep in oxygen-free zones, where they still live today.

Dear Oxygen,

Thanks for destroying the world. We're going to go live in a hole now.

Love, Bacteria

The new photosynthesizing microorganisms, on the other hand, thrived. As a result, atmospheric oxygen rose to half of modern levels by 750 million years ago. Over time, the methane in the atmosphere combined with oxygen to form carbon dioxide. Since this is a weaker greenhouse gas than methane, the earth cooled. Moving continents caused the earth to further cool, and glaciers formed on these continents. Then positive feedback occurred, which is a cycle of cause and effect. In concrete terms, it means that the effects of a cold climate can cause the climate to get even colder. (Or, as we shall see later, the effects of a warm climate can cause the climate to get warmer.) In this case, as ice extended to within 30 degrees of the equator (modern-day Florida), it reflected so much sunlight that the earth cooled enough to allow an ice age referred to as Snowball Earth.

SNOWBALL EARTH!

A severe ice age (with a fun name) overtook the earth 740–580 million years ago. The entire planet may have iced over. With the water cycle shut down, the earth was a cold desert. Then carbon dioxide interrupted the winter fun. Humans weren't around to burn coal, of course. Instead, volcanic eruptions threw carbon dioxide back into the atmosphere, warming the earth and rapidly melting the ice.

Volcanoes are thought to have caused cold climates to warm up in the past, as the eruptions would have released carbon dioxide into the atmosphere.

Now is a good time to address the argument that because climate change occurred before humans existed, global warming must not be caused by humans today. It's true that global warming can occur without human interference. But it also *can* be caused by humans, in the same way that cancer can be caused by both genetic factors and manmade factors, such as tobacco use and water pollution. Through the years, global warming has happened because of the same mechanism: carbon dioxide released into the atmosphere—whether by volcanoes or by the coal we are burning today. Of course, volcanoes still erupt today, but not on a scale that can account for the rising carbon dioxide levels that are being recorded.

At the end of Snowball Earth, the scale of the eruptions was massive, as were the aftereffects. Imagine giant cliffs of ice melting into equally giant waterfalls. It would have been awesome to watch—from a great distance, that is. Luckily nobody was around to see it, and in this instance, global warming was good, as it allowed life to flourish. Phytoplankton had survived under the ice. Now, such plankton thrived, absorbing carbon dioxide and "breathing out" oxygen. With more oxygen in the atmosphere, more complex life could develop.

Approximately 430 million years ago, life emerged from the ocean, and, like a green crayon, colored the shoreline and worked its way up the rivers and farther inland. Moss forests gave way to ferns. Plants were followed by insects, millipedes, and finally vertebrates. Over the millennia, the earth fluctuated between hothouse states (no ice at the poles) and icehouse states (extensive ice at the poles and beyond). Sometimes climate change happened gradually; other times, quickly and catastrophically.

EARTH'S LARGEST MASS EXTINCTION: THE PERMIAN-TRIASSIC

In some cases, climate change led to mass extinctions. We've all learned that an asteroid brought about the demise of the dinosaurs (except for their bird descendants). For a long time, scientists theorized that such collisions had triggered other mass extinctions as well. But no such evidence has been found. Based on the geologic record, scientists now think that the cause of other mass extinctions may have been climate change.

The Permian period came to an end 251 million years ago with an extinction event called the Great Dying. Ninety percent of marine life and 70 percent of land species died. The deep ocean became a dead zone. Scientists have many theories about what led to the catastrophe. One is that massive amounts of lava erupted from several volcanoes on the Siberian continent. The greenhouse gases released by the lava could have caused global warming. Some scientists further theorize that the lava seeped into coal beds. The lava and liquefied coal would have floated to the surface of the earth and reacted to the oxygen in the air, setting off an explosion and sending carbon dioxide from the coal into the atmosphere, a scenario hauntingly similar to the global warming we are causing today by burning coal for power.

Scientists also theorize that when the oceans warmed because of the volcanic eruptions, methane ice may have melted on the ocean floor. When plants are buried in an oxygen-free environment underground, microbes that feed on them produce methane. In cold, high-pressure environments—under permafrost or beneath the ocean slope or ocean floor—methane can combine with water to form methane ice, also known as methane hydrate and methane clathrate. At cold temperatures, it remains solid. But warm water causes the solids to melt, releasing methane gas, a more powerful greenhouse gas than carbon dioxide. The methane escapes the oceans and rises into the atmosphere. In this way, the initial warming caused by massive lava flows would have led to extreme warming caused by melting methane ice.

So why was the deep ocean hit especially hard? Cold and warm water normally interact to form the ocean currents. Currents carry oxygen-rich surface water to the depths of the ocean. The temperature difference in the ocean is what causes ocean water to circulate. As the entire ocean warmed, circulation slowed, and oxygen was no longer carried to the ocean depths. Without oxygen, life in the deep ocean was impossible. This is what caused the oceanic dead zone at the end of the Permian.

The fact that this mass extinction may have been caused

by the initial release of large amounts of carbon dioxide worries scientists, since we are releasing so much carbon dioxide into the atmosphere today. Life did make a comeback, however — in a big way. The Triassic period ushered in the age of the dinosaurs.

THE LAND BEFORE TIME, BUT NOT BEFORE GLOBAL WARMING

Though climate fluctuated during the age of the dinosaurs — and at times there was ice at the poles — it was overall warmer than today, with carbon dioxide levels an estimated two to six times higher. This was due to several factors, including the position of the continents. During the Triassic and Jurassic, the continents were joined together in the supercontinent Pangaea. Large landmasses lead to warmer, drier climates.

Dinosaurs may have also contributed to global warming — not by burning fossil fuels, but simply by passing gas. Grazers like sauropods and cows are able to digest plant matter with the help of microbes in their digestive systems. These microbes create methane, which is released when cows or dinosaurs pass gas. Scientists estimate that the gigantic, gassy sauropods that lived 150 million years ago would have produced 573 million tons (520 million metric tons) of methane each year — which is equivalent to what is produced today by *all* sources of methane.[1] That would have led to some

Jurassic farts? Scientists think that the methane released when herbivorous dinosaurs passed gas may have caused some amount of global warming.

amount of global warming, just as methane contributes to global warming today. Global warming didn't spell the end for the dinosaurs, though. In fact, some scientists think that, having adapted to a hothouse earth climate, the dinosaurs may have become extinct later, in part, due to global cooling.

EXTREME WARMING

The latest incident of extreme warming occurred after the dinosaurs. During a period 58–56 million years ago, global temperatures were already warmer than today. Then, over the course of just a few thousand years, the temperature rose 9 degrees F (5 degrees C). The poles warmed to the point that the Arctic Ocean's summer temperature was the same as today's Jersey Shore waters in August: 74 degrees F (23 degrees C). Tropical seas may have reached hot-tub temperatures of 95–104 degrees F (35–40 degrees C). What caused this warming? Five trillion tons (4.5 trillion metric tons) of carbon dioxide polluted the atmosphere—roughly the same amount as we'll release if we eventually burn through all of our existing coal, oil, and natural gas resources. (If our emissions continue at the current rate, we'll release a whopping three trillion tons within three hundred years.)

Again, people weren't around to burn fossil fuels. As in the Permian-Triassic extinction, scientists think lava flows and melting methane ice may have combined to cause the warming. The already-warm earth would have also caused the positive feedback that releases carbon dioxide, adding to the greenhouse effect. This is the opposite of the positive feedback that led to Snowball Earth, since in this case, a warm climate led to a warmer climate.

As the oceans warmed, just like in the Permian-Triassic extinction, the currents stilled, and in the deep sea, lack of oxygen caused deep-water organisms to die. Land animals suffered from droughts, floods, insect plagues, and food shortages. With less food available, species shrank. For instance, odd as it may sound, horses became the size of housecats. This lasted more than 150,000 years. Then, following nature's usual cycle, greenhouse gases declined, and the earth cooled. Life bounced back. Soon, our own ancestors would make their entrance.

How Do Scientists Know All This?

People have long suspected that the earth's climate changed over time. In the eleventh century, the Chinese scientist Shen Kua discovered fossil bamboo in a dry region of the country. Since bamboo

Glaciers are like a river of ice. They move slowly across the land, carrying with them sediment, rocks, and even large boulders. When the glaciers melt, they leave solid material behind, which is what happened to this rock in Norway, known as a glacial erratic.

thrives in damp conditions, he theorized that the climate must have been more humid in the past. Later, people in the Swiss Alps surmised that the mountain glaciers must have extended farther at one time, based on the contours of the land, and scientists agreed.

Then, in the nineteenth century, the scientist Louis Agassiz constructed the theory of an ice age. Though controversial at the time, it was eventually accepted as the truth.

In the 1980s, scientists were able to definitively link the cold ice-age climate to low greenhouse gas levels. They drilled deep into the Greenland ice sheet and measured carbon dioxide levels in the air that was trapped in the ice more than ten thousand years ago. As suspected, greenhouse gas levels were much lower during the ice age than they are today.

Meanwhile, paleontologists learned that climate and greenhouse gas concentrations had also changed before the ice age. They examined the stomata of fossilized plants. Stomata are the pores through which plants absorb carbon dioxide. Fewer stomata are required when the atmosphere contains more carbon dioxide. So fewer stomata on fossil plant leaves mean there was more carbon dioxide in the air at that time. They also examined the sediment deposited during various eras. Forests leave different deposits than tundra, for instance, and forests indicate a warmer climate than tundra. Further, they could see lava in the sediment record, indicating that volcanoes erupted at certain times, releasing carbon dioxide.

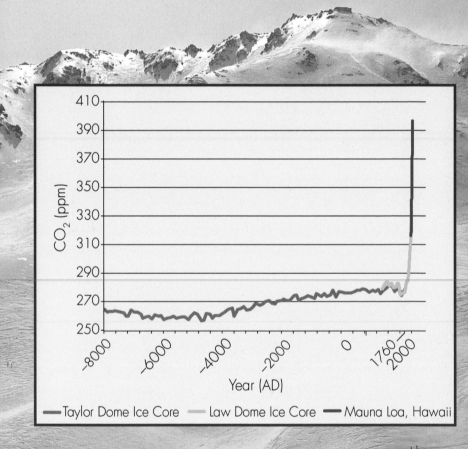

Carbon dioxide levels stayed below 280 parts per million up until the Industrial Revolution, began in 1760, when they began climbing at an alarming rate.

Through these methods, scientists have linked higher concentrations of greenhouse gases with higher temperatures. They have then tested this theory using climate models. Levels of carbon dioxide in the atmosphere consistently explain climate change better than anything else can.

BE THE CHANGE

WHAT: Reduce household emissions.

HOW: Take a quick shower.

WHY: For every five minutes you are in the shower, you use 10 gallons (38 liters) of hot water. It takes a lot of energy to heat that water. In fact, your hot-water heater can use up to 25 percent of your household electricity.

WHAT ELSE: Wash your clothes in cold water to avoid using hot water for the laundry.

CHAPTER 4
RISE OF THE PLANET
OF THE HUMANS

THE FIRST ANCESTORS OF HUMANS, the hominins, evolved five to seven million years ago. They were different from previous apes in that they walked on two legs and eventually were able to make fire, use tools, and plan ahead. These skills would be necessary for surviving an enormous challenge: the ice age.

The Milankovitch cycles, or changes in the earth's position in relation to the sun, triggered the ice age 2.5 million years ago. These changes occur over thousands of years, affecting the way the sun hits the earth. During the ice age, the Milankovitch cycles caused more sunlight to reach the Northern Hemisphere in the winter than in the summer. This produced warmer winters and cooler summers. Although the winters were *warmer* in this scenario, they were not really what we would consider warm. For instance, in what's now Boston, average January lows would have initially ranged from about 22.1 degrees F (–5.5 C) to 31.1 degrees F (–0.5 degrees C).

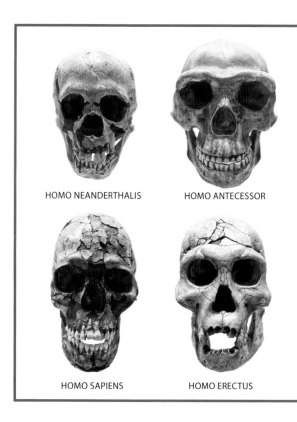

HOMO NEANDERTHALIS

HOMO ANTECESSOR

HOMO SAPIENS

HOMO ERECTUS

Homo sapiens are the only living human species. But in the past, there have been many others, including *Homo neanderthalis, Homo antecessor,* and *Homo erectus.* All of these species walked on two legs, used tools, and had larger (and smarter) brains than their ancestors. Their improved problem-solving skills helped them to cope with the harsh conditions of the ice age.

The relatively warmer winters led to increased snowfall. This is because warming causes increased evaporation, increased moisture in the air, and, thus, increased precipitation. Meanwhile, the cooler summers resulted in less of the snow melting.

The Milankovitch cycles only started the ice age. As more snow accumulated and glaciers expanded, it resulted in positive feedback. For one thing, the glaciers themselves reflected more sunlight than bare land would have. This is because white reflects more sunlight than dark colors (which is why light clothes are cooler to wear in the summer). With sunlight being reflected by the glaciers, the earth was absorbing less heat. The earth cooled, causing less snow to melt and gla-

The Donjek Glacier in Yukon, Canada, is 35 miles (56 kilometers) long. At the peak of the ice age, most of Canada would have been covered with glaciers.

ciers to grow. The expanding glaciers reflected more sunlight, which further cooled the earth, which meant that the glaciers did not melt. Instead, they grew with each winter snowfall. And this cycle continued.

Changes in levels of greenhouse gases were also agents of positive feedback, causing the cold earth to get colder. As the earth cooled, vegetation that would normally rot at the end of its lifecycle froze instead, so that it wasn't releasing carbon dioxide. Also, the cold oceans held more carbon dioxide. For eight hundred thousand years during the ice age, carbon dioxide ranged from 180 parts per million (during the coldest phases, known as glacials) to 280 parts per million (during warmer phases, which are known as interglacials). In contrast, we are now nearing 400 parts per million. With such low carbon dioxide levels during the ice age, the greenhouse effect was weaker than it is today, and so less heat was trapped on earth. Cooling led to more cooling, and the glaciers grew until they covered present-day Alaska, Canada, the upper Midwest and New England, and most of Great Britain, Northern Europe, and Northeast Russia.

Today the opposite is happening. As the earth warms, snow and glaciers are melting, which means less sunlight is being reflected back to space—which in turn contributes to

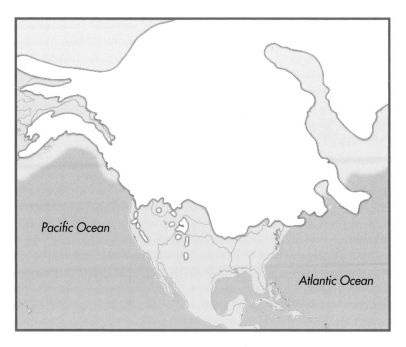

Pacific Ocean

Atlantic Ocean

During the last ice age, glaciers extended into present-day Alaska, Canada, the Upper Midwest, and New England. These glaciers are responsible for many landforms we see today, including the Great Lakes and Cape Cod.

further warming and more snowmelt. As ice melts, vegetation trapped in permafrost (the layer of soil in cold regions that remains permanently frozen) rots, releasing the greenhouse gases carbon dioxide and methane. Meanwhile, warmer oceans release more carbon dioxide into the atmosphere. These greenhouse gases trap more heat, leading to further warming. And this further melts the ice and heats the oceans. In other words, a warming world gets warmer. This is positive feedback too.

When the ice age began, all hominin species still lived in Africa, where glaciers covered only the mountaintops. Still, the ice age affected the continent. During glacial periods, much of the earth's fresh water was locked up in ice, and drought ravaged the land. During these times of drought, the Sahara Desert expanded. Then because of changes in the earth's position relative to the sun and positive feedback, the climate would swing back to warmer temperatures, sometimes within a matter of decades. These interglacial periods changed the ecosystem upon which the hominins had relied for food and water. Hominins' brains grew bigger, possibly as a result of new behavior, such as hunting in packs, which would have helped them to survive in an ever-changing world.

Our species, *Homo sapiens,* evolved from earlier species of hominins about two hundred thousand years ago. Many hominins likely ventured out of Africa through the years. But according to a prominent theory put forth by the anthropologist Stephen Oppenheimer, only one group of perhaps two hundred *Homo sapiens* survived the journey in the long term. The descendants of that group populated the entire world outside of Africa. This global migration was often propelled by crises and opportunities brought about by climate change. For instance, Oppenheimer says that global cooling led to the successful migration out of Africa. Before this migration, 85,000 years ago, people were living as beachcombers along the Red Sea in Africa. With water being trapped in ever-expanding glaciers, sea level dropped 262 feet (80 meters), cutting off the Red Sea from the Indian Ocean. The Red Sea became saltier and plankton declined, along with the shellfish upon which the people had relied. They crossed the Red Sea to the Middle East in search of better beachcombing. From the Middle East, they traveled to Europe, throughout Asia, and eventually into Australia and the Americas.

No matter where humans settled, there was no escaping the harsh conditions of the ice age. Glaciations caused icy deserts in the north and droughts in Africa and Southern Asia. Interglacial periods held dangers of their own, as rapid warming resulted in megafloods. At times the total human population dwindled to ten thousand or less—the size of a large high school. It remained so low, in fact, that our species had little effect on the planet.

The last glacial maximum (the point of greatest ice cover between interglacial periods) occurred approximately twenty thousand years ago. Then the Milankovitch cycles and positive feedback caused the earth to warm again. Melting glaciers unleashed floods containing huge amounts of sediment that had been trapped in ice. This nutrient-rich sediment formed fertile lands. Humans now had the perfect climate—and the perfect soil—needed to create better lives, lives that would allow our population to grow.

THE AGRICULTURAL REVOLUTION

As global temperatures became more predictable, humans who had previously gathered plants and hunted animals instead began to grow plants and raise animals. This shift is known as the Agricultural Revolution. In some cases, migrating people introduced their farming skills to new communities. Other times, farming techniques developed independently. The shift, however, was widespread. Twelve thousand years ago, goats were domesticated in the Middle East. Ten thousand years ago, squash was cultivated in Mexico. By six thousand years ago, rice paddies had been planted in China.

With a steady food supply, the human population grew. This may be when humans first began affecting climate, according to a theory articulated by paleoclimatologist William Ruddiman. Humans burned forests for agricultural land, releasing carbon dioxide. They bred livestock, which increased the number of animals releasing methane. They cultivated rice, which also emits methane. (Rice grows in standing water. Microbes feed on organic matter in this water and release methane. Today, rice farming accounts for 20 percent of global methane emissions.) Other scientists argue that human populations were too small at the time to bring about climate change through agricultural activities. One thing is sure: the growing population caused by the Agricultural Revolution set the stage for our current global warming crisis. Because as our population has expanded, we have used more and more energy, and to keep up with our growing energy needs, we have turned to fossil fuels.

BE THE CHANGE

WHAT: Reduce household emissions.

HOW: In the summer, hang clothes on a clothesline rather than drying them.

WHY: Dryers account for 4 percent of household energy use and contribute 35 million tons (32 million metric tons) of carbon dioxide emissions each year.[2]

WHAT ELSE: Don't automatically throw clothes in the wash after one wear. As a rule of thumb, unless clothes appear or smell dirty, they don't need to be washed. Fewer dirty clothes means fewer wash and dry cycles, which saves money. Also, wash and dry full loads of clothes to get the most out of the energy used by washers and dryers.

EPIC CLIMATE CHANGE

Even after the Agricultural Revolution, humans suffered from famine and war because of short-term climate change. For instance, up until 4,200 years ago, the people of Sumeria (a kingdom in present-day Iraq) had not only survived in a dry climate, but thrived. They used irrigation to farm the arid land, and invented the wheel, the arch, and an advanced system of writing known as cuneiform. A Sumerian poet wrote *The Epic of Gilgamesh,* one of the oldest surviving pieces of literature we have today. Then disaster struck. A two-hundred-year drought forced Sumerians from their homes as livable land shrank by about 93 percent. At around the same time, the capital was attacked by nomads. Though Sumerians didn't disappear entirely, their population declined, their civilization was ravaged, and their language died.

On the other side of the world, the Mayan civilization flourished in present-day Belize, Guatemala, and Mexico between A.D. 300 and 660. Sixty cities of around seventy thousand people each sprang

up during this time, and as in classical Greece, philosophy, politics, and scholarship flourished. Then precipitation decreased. For one thing, the high moisture of the boom years had been unusual. In addition, clearing the forest for cities and agricultural land reduced rainfall. As precipitation decreased and crops failed, the years were marked by famine, war, and migration to coastal areas. By the time the Spanish conquistadors arrived in the 1500s, the once-great Mayan cities had been largely abandoned.

Later on, in Europe, the Little Ice Age lasted from the 1300s to the 1800s. While this wasn't long enough to be considered a glacial period, its effects were devastating: famine in the Northern Hemisphere, Swiss villages destroyed by expanding glaciers, and the death of the first Greenland settlers, who had arrived during a warmer time and weren't prepared for a shortened growing season or the sea ice that prohibited travel to mainland Europe for supplies.

These climate events didn't last long. But for the people living at the time, they were disasters of epic proportions. Because just as humans affect climate, climate affects humans, sometimes altering their quality of life, and other times their ability to survive at all.

CHAPTER 5
HUMANS + FOSSIL FUELS:
A LOVE STORY

Just as the Agricultural Revolution provided a steady food source, the Industrial Revolution improved people's health and quality of life by powering farms, hospitals, schools, and businesses. Unfortunately, it also set the stage for what today threatens our health and quality of life: global warming. Because during the Industrial Revolution, we began relying on fossil fuels.

Coal wasn't the first fuel to contribute to global warming. Until the 1800s, wood was the main source of fuel. It was burned to heat homes and buildings, and to produce steam to power ships and trains. This led to deforestation, a primary cause of greenhouse gas emissions. Also, world population had been rising steadily since the Agricultural Revolution. By 1750, it had reached 750 million people, all of whom needed to be fed and clothed. Trees were chopped down to make way for crops and grazing cattle, further contributing to carbon dioxide emissions. While about 55 percent of these greenhouse gases were absorbed by other plants and the ocean, the rest remains in the air today, and 20 percent of it will persist for thousands of years. Meanwhile, the agricultural lifestyle that had sustained people for thousands of years was no longer viable for the next generation. There were more young people than there were farmland and farm jobs. Many people migrated to cities.

While coal had been burned on a small scale for heat at least since Roman times, it wasn't burned on a large scale until the Industrial Revolution. That's when, in the early 1700s,

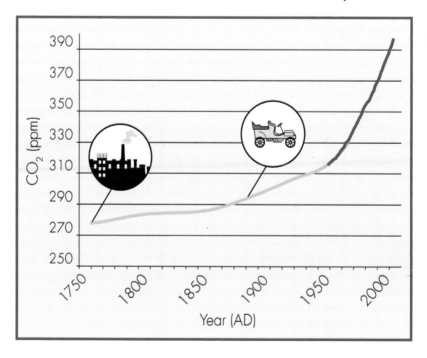

The Industrial Revolution marked the beginning of coal being burned on a large scale. Soon after, the automobile was invented, which led to a reliance on oil for power. And the atmospheric carbon dioxide levels rose and rose.

Abraham Darby invented a coal-fired furnace for smelting iron. Soon, coal was powering the factories that filled the cities, providing jobs to former farmers, but also creating hard lives of working long hours inside polluted factories for little pay. Coal was also causing atmospheric carbon dioxide levels to rise on a dramatic scale. In 1751, only 2.81 million tons (2.55 million metric tons) of carbon dioxide were emitted.[3] By 1900, 588 million tons (533 million metric tons) were being released annually. Today, the figure exceeds 9.9 billion tons (9 billion metric tons). In all, more than 500 billion tons (454 metric tons) of carbon dioxide have been emitted since the start of the Industrial Revolution. Much of the carbon dioxide released more than two hundred years ago still hasn't gone away.

And there would soon be another major contributor to greenhouse gas emissions: oil. In the mid-1800s, Colonel Edwin Drake, a former railroad conductor, went to work for a company that wanted to access the underground oil in Titusville, Pennsylvania. At first Drake tried digging trenches. When that attempt failed, he set about drilling for oil as people at the time drilled for salt deposits. By 1859, Drake had improved his technique so that he became the world's first oil driller. At first, oil was used for lamps, replacing whale oil (and thus saving the whale population, for a while, anyway). Oil lamps were eventually replaced with incandescent light bulbs, which were invented by Thomas Edison for commercial use in 1878. Then coal began to be used for generating electricity

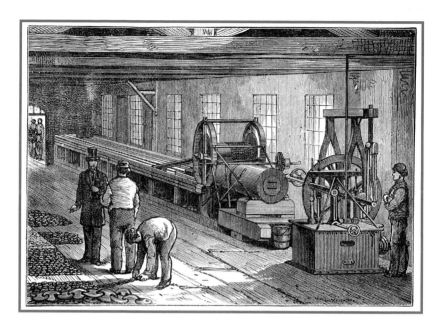

Industrial Revolution machines such as this one were powered by coal. For that reason, carbon dioxide from burning coal began to rise in the 1700s.

in addition to powering factories. Oil joined coal in helping to power electricity, but another new invention would rely on oil as an energy source as well—one that would eventually take the world by storm.

The automobile was invented in 1886, but it wasn't mass-produced until 1908. That's when Henry Ford came out with the Model T, an automobile powered by gasoline, a byprod-uct of oil. During World War I, oil was used to power tanks, trucks, and airplanes. After the war, the number of vehicles used in day-to-day life continued to grow, fueling the need for more and more oil. In 1960, 78.4 percent of households

Thomas Edison was born in 1847. He invented a long-lasting, commercially viable light bulb.

Oil was initially used for lamps. Then people began using light bulbs instead. These were powered by electricity produced by coal.

The Model T, being assembled here by a worker, was the first automobile to be produced on a large scale. Steam and electricity were considered as power sources, but ultimately the car ran on gasoline, a product of oil.

in the United States owned at least one vehicle. By 2011, that percentage had increased to 90.7 percent.

U.S. fuel efficiency standards (regulations that prevent automobiles from guzzling too much gas) were raised from 13.5 to 27.5 miles per gallon (5.7 to 11.7 km/L) in the 1970s but were not raised again until 2007. Congress then passed legislation that would raise fuel efficiency standards to 35 miles per gallon (14.9 km/L) by 2020. A new standard of

54.5 miles per gallon (23.2 km/L) will go into effect in 2025. Meanwhile, low taxes on gasoline in the United States compared with other developed nations did nothing to curb the demand for inefficient vehicles like SUVs — nor the demand for living in inefficient suburbs that are built for driving, not walking or taking public transportation. As a result, in the United States, transportation is responsible for 28 percent of greenhouse gas emissions.

When people began burning coal and oil, all they saw was progress. And this progress was good. Clearing land for farms allowed people to grow food for the world's increasing population. The Industrial Revolution led to cheaper goods and provided jobs for people who could no longer work on farms. Electricity and modern heat reduced the indoor air pollution caused by wood- and coal-burning stoves (pollution that still causes widespread respiratory illness and premature death in developing countries). Electricity led to refrigeration, which better preserves food and is essential for storing the vaccines that prevent illnesses that used to claim the lives of so many children. More efficient transportation thanks to coal-burning trains and oil-burning cars and trucks made it possible to more efficiently exchange goods and ideas. This has allowed the economy to grow, which has lifted people out of poverty worldwide. People didn't know at the time that fossil fuels would change the world in a bad way, too.

But now we know.

BE THE CHANGE

WHAT: Decrease your fuel emissions.

HOW: Set a distance, whether it's a quarter mile, half mile, or mile (0.4, 0.8, or 1.6 kilometers). Walk any distance less than that instead of driving or catching a ride. If you live in a hot or cold climate, set a temperature limit. For instance, you'll walk if it's 20 degrees F (−7 degrees C) or warmer. This will eliminate the excuse that it's too cold when it's really not that cold.

WHY: Transportation is the second biggest contributor to greenhouse gas emissions in America. According to the 2009 National Household Travel Survey, 30 percent of all trips are for 2 miles (3.2 kilometers) or less. If everyone walked some of these short distances, the benefits would add up.

WHAT ELSE: Bike longer distances. Cities are now incorporating more bike lanes into their roads so that bike commutes are easier. Map out the best routes to school, work, and friends' houses and bike instead of drive.

PART THREE
IS IT HOT IN HERE, OR IS IT JUST ME? HOW WE KNOW THE EARTH IS WARMING

CHAPTER 6
THE DISCOVERY OF
GLOBAL WARMING

THAT GLOBAL WARMING IS CAUSED by humans is an older idea than you may think. Irish physicist John Tyndall studied the effects of carbon dioxide on climate in the late 1850s. Tyndall, an alpine climber, was curious about the ice age that created the glaciers in the Alps. Why had the world turned so cold? He theorized that the earth's atmosphere had changed. Scientists understood that the earth's atmosphere must trap heat — otherwise the planet would be much colder — but they didn't know how. Tyndall discovered that carbon dioxide, water vapor, and methane were opaque to infrared rays (heat). That meant the gases absorbed heat, therefore trapping it on Earth rather than allowing it to exit the atmosphere and be lost to space. If the changing atmosphere explained the ice age, these would be the gases that were responsible.

In the 1890s, Svante Arrhenius, a Swedish physicist and Nobel Prize winner for chemistry, further explored the

Global warming isn't a new idea. The Irish physicist John Tyndall began studying the effects of carbon dioxide on climate in the 1850s.

theory that the ice age was caused by lower levels of greenhouse gases in the atmosphere. Arrhenius's math showed that cutting carbon dioxide levels in half would drop temperatures 7–9 degrees F (4–5 degrees C). That's exactly the temperature change that occurred during the ice age. But could the atmospheric levels of carbon dioxide really fluctuate that much?

Arrhenius's colleague, Arvid Högbom, had studied how volcanic eruptions changed carbon dioxide levels in the atmosphere. Now Högbom was examining whether factories were emitting significant levels of carbon dioxide when they burned coal for energy. He learned that factories could emit carbon dioxide in the same way that natural processes did, and he theorized that while carbon dioxide was being added slowly through industry, it would add up over time.

Arrhenius then predicted that if carbon dioxide levels doubled, temperatures would rise 9–11 degrees F (5–6 degrees C). Climate models today predict the same thing. The only difference in the predictions is that Arrhenius thought global warming would occur slowly and be a good thing. The idea that changes in carbon dioxide levels could affect climate remained on the fringe of science for many decades. Most scientists believed Earth's atmosphere to be unchanging.

Then, in the 1950s, U.S. military scientists studying the atmosphere as part of weapons research learned that changes in carbon dioxide levels did, in fact, affect temperature. One such scientist, Gilbert N. Plass, predicted that a doubling of carbon dioxide would lead to a 5.4- to 7.2-degree-F (3- to 4-degree-C) rise in temperature. Some scientists argued that the oceans would absorb any excess carbon dioxide that people were emitting.

To find out if carbon dioxide from fossil fuels was lingering in the atmosphere (as opposed to sinking into the ocean), scientists studied trees. Carbon-14, a radioactive form of carbon, occurs naturally in the environment and also was being released in the 1950s through nuclear bomb testing. Carbon from fossil fuels is different. Because it is millions of years old, it is no longer radioactive. The chemist Hans Suess compared the carbon in trees, and found that some of it was fossil car-

Radioactive carbon-14 occurs naturally in the environment and was also released in the 1950s through nuclear weapons testing. Carbon from burning fossil fuels, on the other hand, is millions of years old and no longer radioactive. This difference has allowed scientists to study how much carbon dioxide from fossil fuels is being absorbed by trees.

bon. The newer the trees were, the higher the ratio of fossil carbon to carbon-14. This proved that carbon dioxide from burning fossil fuels was showing up in the atmosphere (and thus being absorbed by trees).

Next, Suess worked with the scientist Roger Revelle to study how the oceans were absorbing carbon dioxide. Revelle found that the oceans could absorb only a fraction of the carbon dioxide emitted. He predicted that over time, increasing levels of carbon dioxide in the atmosphere could change our climate dramatically. Scientists began to seriously consider the possibility of global warming, but they needed accurate measurements of the amount of carbon dioxide being released into the atmosphere.

To that end, the scientist Charles David Keeling, working for Revelle and Suess, established a carbon dioxide measuring station in Mauna Loa, Hawaii, in the late 1950s. Within two years, measurements showed a rise in carbon dioxide—the famous ascending jagged line (jagged because plants in the Northern Hemisphere—where the bulk of all landmass is—grow during the spring and summer, allowing them to absorb carbon dioxide, and decay in the fall and winter, causing them to release carbon dioxide).

Scientists in diverse fields, including biology, geochemistry, and atmospheric science, began discussing carbon dioxide in the atmosphere and its effect on climate. In the late 1960s, scientists, including Syukuro Manabe at the National Oceanic and Atmospheric Administration (NOAA) and James Hansen at NASA, created climate models that indicated how the climate would change as more carbon dioxide was added to the atmosphere. The results of these models caused the then-president Jimmy Carter to call on the National Academy of Sciences, America's leading scientific body, to investigate.

In 1979, Jule Charney, a meteorologist from the Mas-

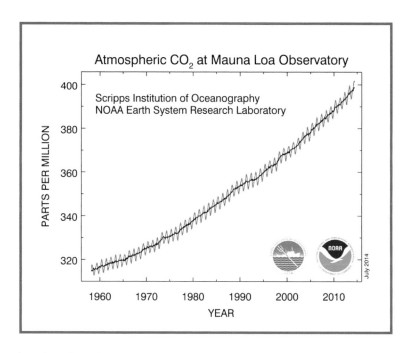

Atmospheric CO$_2$ at Mauna Loa Observatory

Scripps Institution of Oceanography
NOAA Earth System Research Laboratory

Carbon dioxide in the atmosphere has been measured at a station in Mauna Loa, Hawaii, since the late 1950s. Since then, the amount of carbon dioxide has increased year after year. The line is jagged because plants absorb carbon dioxide in the spring and summer, and release it when they decay in the fall and winter.

sachusetts Institute of Technology, led the Ad Hoc Study Group on Carbon Dioxide and Climate. The panel found the climate models to be accurate, stating, "If carbon dioxide continues to increase, the study finds no reason to doubt that climate change will result and no reason to believe that these changes will be negligible." The panel predicted a 2.5-degree-F (1.4-degree-C) rise in global temperature with a doubling of mid-nineteenth-century carbon dioxide levels. Many studies have since confirmed these results.

Meanwhile, confirmation regarding the importance of carbon dioxide to climate came in the 1980s from ice samples. Scientists drilled deep into the ice sheets in Greenland and Antarctica. By crushing sections of the ice and measuring the carbon dioxide released, they were able to determine the levels of carbon dioxide during the last ice age. As predicted by Arrhenius so long ago, carbon dioxide levels were about 50 percent lower during the ice age than in the 1980s. Further, scientists found that carbon dioxide levels had gone up during interglacial periods and down during glacial periods as a result of positive feedback.

In 1988, the United Nations created the Intergovernmental Panel on Climate Change (IPCC) to study global warming. Since then, thousands of scientists worldwide have worked on the panel to publish five major assessment reports, most recently in 2013. The panel assesses global warming as it happens, and predicts possible outcomes of global warming according to various levels of carbon dioxide emitted. These reports have consistently said that climate change is happening and is caused by people.

There is no longer any doubt that we are affecting the climate.

BE THE CHANGE

WHAT: Decrease your fuel emissions.

HOW: Carpool or take public transportation.

WHY: Every gallon of gasoline your car burns releases 20 pounds (9 kilograms) of carbon dioxide into the air. (The carbon dioxide released weighs more than the actual gasoline because the carbon from the gasoline combines with oxygen from the air.) If your car gets about 20 miles per gallon (7 kilometers per liter), then for every mile you carpool, you prevent 1 pound (0.45 kilograms) of carbon dioxide from entering the air (or more if you carpool with two or more people). Public transportation is like a giant carpool, in which you can divide your fuel or electricity use by ten, twenty, fifty, or even hundreds of other people.

WHAT ELSE: Even better, arrange a walking or biking carpool. If you have a buddy to walk with, you're more likely to stick to your walking routine.

CHAPTER 7
THE EVIDENCE TODAY

To SEE IF THE EARTH is warming, it makes sense to take its temperature. Global temperatures were recorded beginning in the mid-1800s. Since then, scientists have recorded a 1.4-degree-F (0.85-degree-C) increase in the global temperature, according to the 2013 IPCC report. Nine out of ten of the warmest years on record have occurred since 2000, and 2012 was the warmest year on record for the United States. Overall, there has been a decrease in cold days and nights, and an increase in warm days and nights.

Now, I'm writing this during a winter when record lows have been set, thanks to a polar vortex pushing Arctic winds to the south. Some people took this as evidence that global warming wasn't happening. But it makes sense that even with global warming, we would have cold winters. The temperature has increased less than 1.8 degrees F (1 degree C). But from year to year, average seasonal temperatures can vary by more than 18 degrees F (10 degrees C). For instance, in

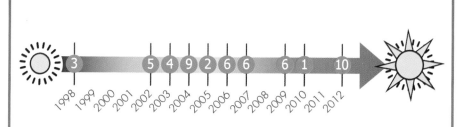

Rank: 1 = warmest
Note: 2006, 2007, and 2009 tied for the 6th warmest
Source: NOAA

Ten of the warmest years on record have occurred since 1998.

Kansas City, the warmest winter season on record averaged 39 degrees F (4 degrees C), and the coolest, 21 degrees F (-6 degrees C). Seasons will still vary from year to year, but with global warming there will tend to be more warm seasons. Likewise, record lows will still be set, but not as often, whereas record highs have always been set, but will now be set *more* often.

While a degree F doesn't feel like much from day to day, evidence shows that it has a pronounced effect on climate. The IPCC states that climate change *currently* contributes to premature death through disease, weather events, poorer water, air, and food quality, and changes in ecosystems, agriculture, industry, and settlements. The World Health Organization blamed 140,000 premature deaths yearly beginning in 2004 on global warming. The Global Humanitarian Forum, led by former UN Secretary General Kofi Annan, went

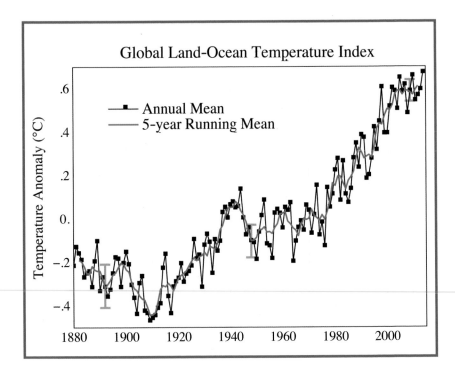

Global Land-Ocean Temperature Index

"If global warming is happening, then why is it so freakin' cold this winter?" Most of us have heard this or a similar question. It's because the average winter temperature in a particular place varies widely from year to year. Global warming, on the other hand, is occurring in much smaller increments from year to year. As you can see from this graph, the global temperature has gone up and down slightly, but overall has been increasing since at least the early 1920s.

further, saying that global warming caused 300,000 premature deaths per year, and that 99 percent of those occurred in developing nations that contribute less than 1 percent of the world's greenhouse gas emissions. The consequences of climate change will continue to grow. But they're already happening right now.

ARCTIC MELTDOWN

As climate models have predicted, the poles are warming more quickly than the rest of the earth. Temperatures in West Antarctica have risen 4.3 degrees F (2.4 degrees C) since the 1950s.[4] The Arctic is 3.6 degrees F (2 degrees C) warmer than it was in the mid-1960s, and in some parts, summer temperatures have risen a whopping 11 degrees F (6 degrees C). This is because melting snow and ice are lowering the Arctic's ability to reflect sunlight, causing it to absorb more of the sun's heat.

Signs of rapid warming in the Arctic include declining spring snow and melting permafrost. Snow cover during the month of June dropped 11.7 percent per decade from 1967 to 2012,[5] and there hasn't been an increase in any month during that time. Since early 1980, permafrost has warmed up 5.4 degrees F (3 degrees C) in northern Alaska, and up to 3.6 degrees F (2 degrees C) in Northern Europe and Russia. This is a good measure of global warming because permafrost temperature is more constant than air temperature. As the permafrost temperature rises, it melts. In Alaska, this has led to unstable homes as the ground rots beneath them.

Rotting permafrost is also creating a positive feedback loop. Carbon and methane are stored in the permafrost as frozen dead plant matter. In the Arctic, the upper 10 feet (3 meters) of permafrost store more than twice as much car-

The Arctic and Antarctica are warming more quickly than the rest of the earth. The Arctic, for instance, is 3.6 degrees F (2 degrees C) warmer than it was in the mid-1960s.

bon as the atmosphere contains today.[6] As the permafrost rots, carbon dioxide and methane are released into the atmosphere. In Sweden, for instance, permafrost in a bog known as the Stordalen Mire is releasing as much as 60 percent more methane than it was thirty-five years ago.[7]

SHRINKING SEA ICE

Sea ice is also shrinking. Multi-year ice, which doesn't melt even through Arctic summers, is shrinking by 17.2 percent per decade, according to NASA. Sea ice does not contribute to a rise in sea level, as sea ice is already *in* the ocean. However, it can still cause flooding along coasts, as the people of Shishmaref, Alaska, can tell you.

Over the centuries, the sea ice had protected Shishmaref,

Due to global warming, the Arctic sea ice is shrinking. The red line outlines the extent of the sea ice in 1979, compared to today.

a fishing and seal-hunting island just about 4 miles (6.4 kilometers) long, from storm surges. (Storm surges are rises of sea level that occur during a storm because of wind and atmospheric pressure.) With the ice forming later in the fall and melting earlier in the spring, storm surges have inundated the town. In 1997, a storm destroyed 125 feet (38 meters) of land. A 2001 storm brought 12-foot (3.7-meter) waves. Foreseeing repeated flooding, the people of Shishmaref plan to relocate their entire village, at a cost of $180 million. Other seaside Alaskan villages are facing the same problem.

In 2005, the people of Shishmaref and other Inuit groups filed a complaint with the Inter-American Commission on Human Rights stating that the United States is causing global warming and thus destroying the Inuit way of life, and their property and livelihood. In 2008, the town of Kivalina, Alaska, sued U.S. oil, gas, and power companies for their role in global warming. If such lawsuits become commonplace, failing to take action to stop global warming could become expensive for governments and businesses.

Ironically, the melting polar ice cap is opening new oil and gas reserves. The United States Geological Survey estimates that one-fourth of the world's undiscovered oil and gas lie under the Arctic Ocean. The melting Arctic Sea also promises valuable new shipping routes. For these reasons, Canada, Denmark, the United States, Norway, and Russia are vying for territory in the Arctic Sea. In 2007, Russian explorers even planted a flag in the seabed at the North Pole to stake their nation's claim, which was later disputed by other countries. Increased greenhouse gas emissions due to burning oil found beneath the melting Arctic Sea would cause a positive feedback loop that would be particularly hard to stomach.

MELTING GLACIERS

As the world warms, glaciers are retreating at the poles and elsewhere. Worldwide, they are losing 303 gigatons (275 metric gigatons) of ice per year, according to the 2013 IPCC report. (One gigaton is one billion tons.) Climate models predict that glaciers in Montana's Glacier National Park will vanish by 2030 and that Iceland will be nearly ice-free by 2200. Scientists are particularly concerned about Greenland and Antarctica, home to the only glaciers large enough to be called ice sheets. Together, they hold 99 percent of the world's freshwater glacier ice, and they're losing mass faster with each decade. In Greenland, ice melted at a rate of 37.5 gigatons (34 metric gigatons) per year from 1992 to 2001, but the rate increased to 237 gigatons (215 metric gigatons) per year from 2002 to 2011. In Antarctica, the rate increased from 33 gigatons (30 metric gigatons) per year to 162 gigatons (147 metric gigatons) per year during the same time frame.

There are two big problems caused by melting glaciers. First, mountain glaciers store fresh water. During dry, hot months, the ice melts into rivers and streams, which are used for irrigation and hydropower. When glaciers melt due to global warming, the meltwater gushes into the ocean instead, cutting down the fresh water supply available each summer. Second, glacial meltwater causes a rise in sea level. If

Dawes Glacier in Alaska calves, meaning that chunks of ice break off its edge. While calving is a natural process, some calving is due to the fact that glaciers are shrinking worldwide as the earth warms.

the Greenland ice sheet melted completely, it would result in a 23-foot (7-meter) rise in sea level. An ice-free Antarctica would cause a further 197-foot (60-meter) rise in sea level. Antarctica is less vulnerable to ice melt than the Arctic. This is because Antarctica is a continent that spans the South Pole, whereas the Arctic is an ocean that spans the North Pole. Ice on land melts less easily than sea ice. (In fact, the sea ice surrounding Antarctica melts each summer.) Antarctica is also colder than the Arctic because of the continent's high elevation (which averages 7,500 feet, or 2,286 meters). The air gets colder at higher elevations, which is why Colorado has a cooler climate than neighboring Kansas. Because it is so very cold in Antarctica, slight warming will not change things as drastically as it does in the Arctic. However, as global warming continues, scientists predict that the West Antarctic ice sheet will melt, resulting in an additional 16-foot (5-meter) sea level rise.

RISING SEA LEVEL

Worldwide, sea level has risen 7.5 inches (19 centimeters) between 1901 and 2010, according to the 2013 IPCC Report. The average rate should be 0.07 inches (1.7 millimeters) per year, but the rate has increased through the years so that between 1993 and 2010, the sea level rose 0.13 inches (3.2 millimeters) per year, or a little over an inch each decade. This rise comes from meltwater from glaciers, along with thermal expansion due to warming. (Warm ocean water takes up more space than cold water because the molecules in warm water move around more quickly, bumping into each other and causing the water to expand.)

Whole countries are now at risk of being inundated by the tides, including the Pacific island nations of Tuvalu, Kiribati, Tokelau, Tonga, Fiji, Somoa, and Maldives. Already, tides are coming in farther, storm surges are becoming more frequent, islets are disappearing, and soil is becoming waterlogged. In Tuvalu, landmarks that used to be on dry soil are now 20 feet (6 meters) offshore. The government hopes to move its twelve thousand people to Australia should they become some of the first global warming refugees. To move an entire

A graveyard in Majuro Atoll (part of the Marshall Islands, just north of Tuvalu) is flooded during high tide and ocean surges. Many Pacific islands are only about three feet above sea level, and they are gradually being swallowed by the rising sea.

country across the ocean would cost millions of dollars. The people would suffer a loss of community and cultural identity that comes from being uprooted from one's homeland. And other countries are often reluctant to accept refugees because they require jobs, housing, food, and medical aid—all costly investments. So to consider such a move shows that the government of Tuvalu, like that of Kiribati and others, believes its situation is dire indeed.

STORMS AND FLOODS

Warmer air causes more water evaporation, and increased water vapor leads to bigger storms. Florida was hit by four hurricanes in 2004, more than any state since 1886. The following year, there were a record-breaking thirteen hurricanes worldwide, including Hurricane Katrina in New Orleans and the Gulf Coast. Economic losses from these storms totaled $200 billion. More recently, Hurricane Sandy, an unusual storm in terms of size and how it made landfall, blasted New York and New Jersey in 2012, killing more than one hundred, knocking out power in more than eight million homes, and costing $25 billion. The following year, Boulder, Colorado, was struck with a thousand-year flood (meaning that statistically it should happen only once in a thousand years), after getting 15 inches (38 centimeters) of rainfall in a week (the average *yearly* rainfall in this area is 20 inches, or 51 centimeters).

It is difficult to peg specific weather events like these on global warming, because they have always occurred, some years more than others. However, as the number of storms increases, they can't all be chalked up to flukes of nature. On November 8, 2013, Super Typhoon Haiyan was one of the strongest ever to make landfall. It killed more than 5,700 people and left 2.5 million in urgent need of food. The UN chief Ban Ki-moon pulled no punches in blaming the storm

Hurricane Katrina killed 1,833 people and left many others homeless.

Steps are all that remain of this New Orleans home after storm surges during Hurricane Katrina caused catastrophic flooding.

A mother and her two children walk past a ship that ran aground during Typhoon Haiyan. The storm, which killed more than 5,700, has been blamed on global warming.

A storm surge during Superstorm Sandy took out Casino Pier in Seaside Heights, New Jersey. The pier was home to the Jet Star roller coaster, which wound up in the Atlantic Ocean and became a symbol of the storm. In a survey, many people said Superstorm Sandy made them think of global warming as a current problem, not just a future one.

on global warming. "We have seen now what has happened in the Philippines," he said prior to climate talks in Poland. "It is an urgent warning, an example of changed weather and how climate change is affecting all of us on earth." The stakes of creating conditions that are conducive to such storms are high everywhere, but especially in developing nations, where 95 percent of all deaths from natural disasters occur, according to the 2007 IPCC report.

HEAT WAVES AND DISEASE

Not surprisingly, a major effect of global warming is heat. In 2013, Australia had its worst heat wave on record. The same year, China endured its worst heat wave in 140 years. A heat wave in Russia in 2010 killed fifty-six thousand people. And more than thirty-five thousand died in the 2003 heat wave in Europe.

In addition to causing heat exhaustion, the warmer climate is leading to the spread of tropical diseases. Cases of malaria, dengue fever, and encephalitis are spreading to higher and lower latitudes, and to higher altitudes, which typically have cooler temperatures. For instance, in Mexico, dengue fever expanded into the northern state of Chihuahua, and nationwide, cases increased more than 600 percent from 2001 to 2007.[8] Throughout the Americas, the number of dengue fever cases increased from 66,000 to 552,000 in a span of twenty-six years. Rising temperatures and increased rainfall are to blame.

DROUGHTS AND WILDFIRES

While storms increase with heat, so do droughts. Warm air dries land faster, leading to droughts in already arid regions. Since the 1970s, land area with drought conditions has more than doubled, according to the 2007 IPCC report. Africa has been particularly susceptible. And in poor nations, where little or no aid is provided to farmers and herders when their crops fail or cattle die, droughts are deadly. In 2011, the worst drought in sixty years forced tens of thousands of Somalis to

Somalian children fetch water at the Dadaab refugee camp in Kenya in 2011. They were forced to seek assistance in the neighboring country because their home country was facing the worst drought in sixty years. Droughts have become much more widespread due to global warming, and Africa has been hit especially hard.

cross the desert to reach a Kenyan refugee camp. Many never made it, and of those who did, many were on the brink of starving to death.

In Australia, a decade-long drought beginning in 2000 caused dust storms, wildfires, and water shortages as the Murray River shrank until it no longer reached the sea. Crops failed, and the sheep population declined by 50 percent. Thousands of families gave up farming altogether. Sci-

The U.S. wildfire season is two months longer than it was in the early 1970s, resulting in loss of property and sometimes lives.

entists believe a similar situation could occur in the American Southwest, and in fact, drought overtook 55 percent of America in 2012, the most area since 1956.

Warmer and drier conditions due to global warming have

intensified wildfires. In the U.S. West, the wildfire season is two months longer than it was in the early 1970s, according to testimony by Forest Service Chief Tom Tidwell before a U.S. Senate committee in 2013. This is because warmer summers lead to drier conditions conducive to wildfires. They also lead to the proliferation of insects that eat—and kill—trees, which become kindling for wildfires.

SPECIES AT RISK

Throughout the world, animal and plant species have been

Plants and animals have adapted to the present climate. As the climate warms, they are moving toward the poles, unless they are hindered by human settlement. Animals that already live in the Arctic, such as polar bears, have nowhere to go to seek a cooler climate for their survival.

affected by climate change. The National Wildlife Federation says that 60 percent of the birds they track have moved an average of 35 miles (56 kilometers) north in forty years. The comma butterfly has migrated 130 miles (209 kilometers) north over the past forty years. Plant species are also migrating. Taller shrubs are appearing in tundra as a result of global warming. In general, as their homelands warm, plants and animals are moving toward the cooler poles if they can. This migration is difficult because people have settled so many wild lands that, in many cases, wildlife is trapped in its present habitats.

Meanwhile, animals at the poles have nowhere to go to find a colder climate. Polar bears have become the poster child for global warming, and for good reason: they hunt on and around sea ice. Seals are right there with polar bears, though, in terms of impact. Mother seals give birth and nurse their pups on spring sea ice. As Arctic sea ice melts earlier in the spring, baby seals are losing their icy safe havens, without which they cannot survive. As the seal population decreases, polar bears are losing their primary food source. And that is negatively impacting their health and reproduction rates.

OCEAN WARMING AND ACIDIFICATION

Changes are under way in our oceans, too. Between one-fourth and one-half of the carbon dioxide emitted by humans winds up in the ocean. This is good in that it scrubs carbon dioxide from the atmosphere, but it's at the expense of ocean life. Carbon dioxide reacts with water to form carbonic acid. As carbon dioxide in the ocean increases, so do levels of carbonic acid, so that the pH level of the ocean has changed from 8.2 to 8.1 in the last century. A single decimal point change may seem minor, but the pH scale only ranges from 0 to 14. (The most acidic is 0, the most basic is 14, and 7 is neutral.) So a 0.1 increase in acidity is actually a big change.

This change in the ocean's chemistry also has big consequences. Because carbonic acid corrodes shells and negatively impacts the shell-building of mollusks, there is an expected decrease in shelled zooplankton (microscopic animals). This will be coupled with a decrease in phytoplankton already occurring in the ocean as it warms. With plankton at the base of the food chain, this will cause a ripple effect throughout the oceans.

Global warming is also affecting coral reefs in a process called coral "bleaching." Corals get their color from the algae that live inside polyps (the name for individual coral animals). Corals rely on the algae for nutrition. But under stress, corals will expel the algae and turn white—then they die. Corals have adapted to a steady ocean temperature. Rapid warming, along with acidification and pollution, is causing the corals stress, which has contributed to widespread coral bleaching. An estimated 27 percent of coral reefs have already been lost. This takes a heavy toll on marine life, as 25 percent of all species spend at least part of their lives in the reefs. The ripple effect will also reach the three billion people who rely on the ocean for their livelihoods.

Global warming is often described as an environmental crisis, and it is. But as you can see from the changes already under way with just 1.4 degrees F (0.85 degrees C) of warming, it is even more so a humanitarian crisis. People are losing their homes, their water sources, and their abilities to make a living. And in the case of climate change, not only are people suffering because of the crisis—we are also the ones causing it.

BE THE CHANGE

WHAT: Reduce your fuel emissions.

HOW: If you drive, keep your vehicle well maintained.

WHY: Ensuring that you have adequate air in your tires can increase your mileage by 3 percent, reducing the amount of fuel you burn. (Think about it: riding a bicycle becomes harder as the tires contain less air; it's the same idea with cars.) Regular tune-ups and repairs can make your car up to 7 percent more fuel efficient.

WHAT ELSE: In the summer, parking in the shade and driving along shady routes can reduce your air conditioning use, also reducing the amount of fuel you use.

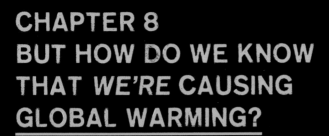

CHAPTER 8
BUT HOW DO WE KNOW
THAT *WE'RE* CAUSING
GLOBAL WARMING?

SCIENTISTS DIFFERENTIATE THE GLOBAL WARMING happening today from climate change of the past by calling it anthropogenic (human-caused) climate change. How do we show that today's climate change is anthropogenic, and not caused by some other factor? We know from physics that burning fossil fuels releases carbon dioxide into the air, and that increased carbon dioxide in the air magnifies the greenhouse effect, causing warming. To prove that this is, in fact, what is happening, we would need to show that carbon dioxide has been on the rise since the Industrial Revolution, and that with it, the global temperature has also risen. That's exactly what the data have shown.

Greenhouse gas levels have been measured at atmospheric data stations across the world since the 1950s. Scientists measure earlier carbon dioxide levels through ice samples taken from glaciers in the Arctic and Antarctica. Based on these data, we know that from at least eight hundred thousand years ago up to the Industrial Revolution, carbon dioxide levels had stayed below 280 parts per million (often averaging just 180 parts per million during the coldest periods of the ice age). Since the Industrial Revolution, carbon dioxide has risen from 280 parts per million to 396 parts per million in 2013. Current levels are the highest in three million years. Meanwhile, global temperature has already risen 1.4 degrees F (0.85 degrees C) since 1880.

Scientists have concluded that humans are causing global

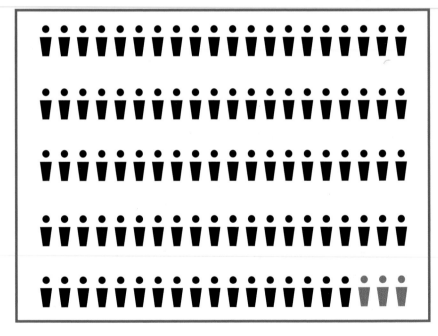

Ninety-seven out of 100 peer-reviewed science articles that state a position on global warming say that it is a result of human activity.

warming. This conclusion is based on a few factors. It's a fact that greenhouse gases began rising at the onset of the Industrial Revolution. It's also a fact that the burning of coal and oil releases carbon dioxide into the atmosphere. Based on fundamental physics, greenhouse gases like carbon dioxide trap heat, and because scientists have seen that the average global temperature has risen in the past century, they can analyze all of this data and conclude that human beings are causing global warming.

But how can we be sure? We know from the geologic record that carbon dioxide has had a great influence on climate. Current climate models also show carbon dioxide's important role. Remove carbon dioxide from climate models, and you get Snowball Earth. Leave out human effects on models, and warming does not occur. Further, the influence of greenhouse gases on temperature is now testable by measuring temperatures in the upper and lower atmospheres. The sun heats up all strata in the atmosphere. With greenhouse gas warming, only the lower strata warm up. The upper strata cool down. And that is what NASA data show to be happening.

Based on this and other evidence, more than eight hundred leading climate scientists from around the world stated in the 2013 IPCC report that global warming is happening, is caused by humans, and is responsible for melting ice, rising sea level, and many weather extremes. But are all scientists in agreement? The overwhelming majority are.

Scientists publish articles in journals to report their findings on climate change (and other areas of study). To be published, each article must be reviewed by other scientists to ensure accuracy. In a recent study done by John Cooke and published in the journal *Environmental Research Letters*, 11,944 articles published in peer-reviewed journals were analyzed. Of those articles, 66.4 percent stated no position on whether global warming was occurring as a result of humans. That is to be expected on a topic with such a wide consensus. Scientists writing about medical factors that could explain the Salem witch trials, for instance, would feel no need to state that the girls who accused the residents of Salem of witchcraft hadn't really been bewitched. Of the scientific articles that did take a position on global warming, 97.1 percent of them said that global warming was a result of human activity. Now, a skeptic could ask about the other 2.9 percent. That's certainly a good question. But when it comes to taking action, with the fate of millions of people in the balance, it would be wise to heed the advice of the 97 percent. To put it in personal terms, if you went to see 100 doctors, and 97 told you that you needed surgery to save your life, you would likely heed the advice of that overwhelming majority.

To be sure, there are many news pundits, scientists hired as experts by greenhouse gas polluters (more on that later), politicians, and probably people you know who will state that global warming isn't occurring or isn't caused by humans. But remember, anyone can have an opinion. In the field of science, hypotheses have to be tested and proven beyond a reasonable doubt to be true. When it comes to global warming and whether or not it's being caused by human actions, the verdict is in.

There is no reasonable doubt.

BE THE CHANGE

WHAT: *Reduce agricultural emissions.*

HOW: *Eat one less beef or dairy meal per week.*

WHY: *Raising animals, and particularly cattle, produces greenhouse gas emissions in a number of ways, including the methane produced in their manure and gas. Switching from beef or dairy to chicken or fish for one meal per week would reduce your greenhouse gas emissions the equivalent of driving 760 miles (1,230 kilometers) less over the course of the year. Switching from beef or dairy to vegetables for one meal would be the equivalent of driving 1,160 miles (1,860 kilometers) less per year.[9]*

WHAT ELSE: *Grow your own favorite fruit or vegetable. Do you like salad? Grow lettuce. Enjoy veggies and dip? Grow carrots. Love pie? Grow a cherry tree. Though seeds or starter plants cost money up front, you will save in the long run, especially if you use your own nutrient-rich soil from composting. This idea isn't just for house dwellers. If you live in an apartment, herbs and some vegetables can be grown in pots. Growing your own produce reduces emissions because food shipped across the country—or from another country—adds to carbon dioxide emissions. Growing your own fruit or vegetables reduces these emissions.*

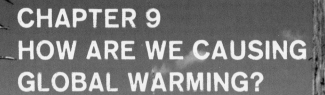

CHAPTER 9
HOW ARE WE CAUSING GLOBAL WARMING?

IT's AN ESTABLISHED FACT THAT humans are causing global warming through our greenhouse gas emissions. But how exactly is that happening? The Environmental Protection Agency (EPA) states that the top greenhouse gases being emitted globally are carbon dioxide (77 percent), methane (14 percent), nitrous oxide (8 percent), and fluorinated gases (1 percent). Water vapor is left out of this breakdown, since it fluctuates hourly and daily and is not seen as an instigator of climate change. Rather, it is an example of positive feedback. A warmer climate causes more water to evaporate, trapping more heat. In the United States, carbon dioxide is also the leading greenhouse gas, making up 84 percent of the total greenhouse gases emitted.

Carbon dioxide is emitted during the burning of fossil fuels by vehicles, power plants, and industry. Carbon dioxide from fossil fuels accounts for 57 percent of all greenhouse gas emissions. Carbon dioxide from deforestation, industrial

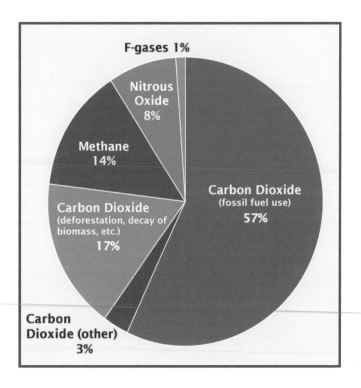

Carbon dioxide comprises 77 percent of all greenhouse gases emitted worldwide.

chemical reactions, and other factors accounts for another 20 percent.

Though less prevalent than carbon dioxide, **methane** is twenty-one times more effective pound for pound at heating the atmosphere. And it has more than doubled since preindustrial times.[10] Methane is released by rotting plants and animals. If oxygen is present, bacteria decompose the remains and produce carbon dioxide. But in oxygen-free environments, microbes called methanogens consume the organisms and produce methane. In this way, methane is emitted

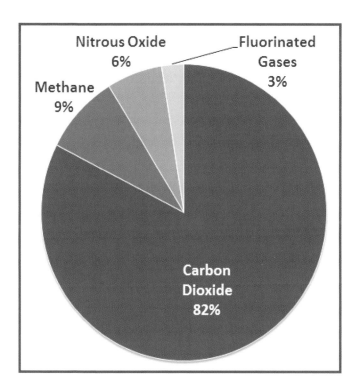

In the United States, carbon dioxide makes up 82 percent of all greenhouse gases emitted.

by rotting organic waste in landfills, leaky sewage lines, manure, and cow gas. It's also released during the production and transportation of fossil fuels.

Nitrous oxide is three hundred times more potent than carbon dioxide as a greenhouse gas. Sixty-nine percent of its emissions are due to the management of agricultural soil, and especially the use of synthetic fertilizer. Other sources include livestock manure and urine, fossil fuels, and industry.

Fluorinated gases, or F-gases, refer to several gases, which vary in potency. Though they make up only a small percentage of greenhouse gas emissions, they are anywhere from 140 to a whopping 23,900 times better at trapping heat than carbon dioxide. F-gases were substituted in products for chlorofluorocarbons, which were banned internationally when it was discovered that they were depleting the ozone. F-gases are now found in refrigerants, aerosol propellants, and fire retardants. They are also emitted during industrial processes, such as aluminum production.

Water vapor is the most abundant greenhouse gas, but is less talked about because people don't directly add water vapor to the atmosphere. Instead, it's all about the water cycle. Water from lakes, rivers, and oceans is evaporated into the air, where it becomes a gas—water vapor. Later it may change back into liquid in the form of clouds. While it is water vapor, it traps heat in the atmosphere just as carbon dioxide does. As the earth warms, it will cause more water to evaporate, and that added water vapor could increase the warming effect—yet another example of positive feedback.

Black carbon, or black soot, is not a gas but a solid. However, it traps heat in the atmosphere just as greenhouse gases do. Black carbon is second only to carbon dioxide as a cause of global warming.[11] Because black carbon darkens snow and ice, reducing the reflection of sunlight, it contributes to rapid warming in the Arctic. Sources of black carbon include forest fires, landfill fires, diesel engine exhaust, and wood-burning and coal-burning stoves used for heating and cooking. Because black soot pollution is a known cause of lung cancer, reducing it in the atmosphere would not only slow global warming; it would also prevent disease.

WHERE ON EARTH DO ALL THESE GREENHOUSE GAS EMISSIONS COME FROM?

China leads all other nations in greenhouse gas emissions, followed by the United States, the European Union, India, Russia, Japan, and Canada. It should be noted that the Unit-

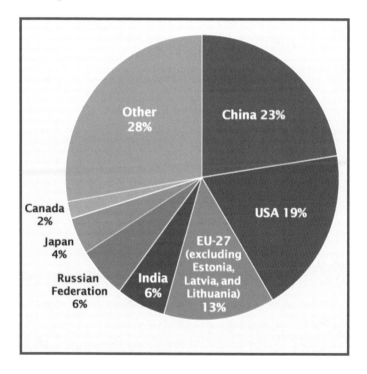

China and the United States are the leading greenhouse gas emitters by country.

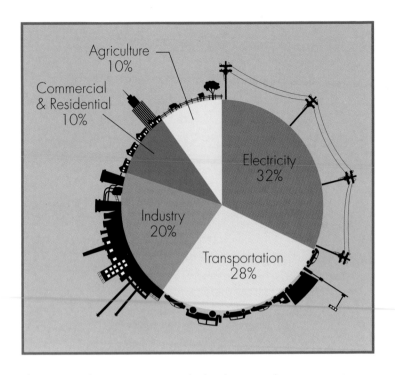

Electricity and transportation are the leading greenhouse gas emitters in America because both rely on fossil fuels.

ed States emits much more carbon dioxide per person than China, 19.4 tons (17.6 metric tons) per person in 2010, compared with 6.8 tons (6.2 metric tons) per person in China.[12] The United States is surpassed by other nations in per capita carbon dioxide emissions, including Qatar, Kuwait, and the United Arab Emirates. However, emissions in the United States are of particular concern because it is the third most populous country in the world.

Globally, electricity and heat are the top sources of greenhouse gas emissions, according to the EPA. Next comes industry—the emissions released in the process of making goods—followed by forestry. In the United States, it's a different story. Electricity is still the leading emitter of greenhouse gases. But transportation takes second place. Forestry doesn't even make the list. That's because conservation efforts in America have resulted in forests, grasslands, wetlands, and other wild lands absorbing 14 percent more greenhouse gases than are emitted by the clearing of these wild lands.

Now, if we look at companies instead of countries, the

Sixty-three percent of the carbon dioxide and methane released from 1751 to 2010 were emitted by just ninety companies.

world gets a lot smaller. According to a study in the journal *Climate Change,* 63 percent of the carbon dioxide and methane released from 1751 to 2010 was emitted by just ninety companies. All but seven are oil, coal, or gas companies, including Chevron, Exxon, BP, and several government-owned oil and coal companies. The seven non-energy companies were cement companies.

So how is this small group of companies making such a negative impact? Through the burning of fossil fuels.

ELECTRICITY AND COAL

Electricity and heat combined are the leading sources of greenhouse gas emissions worldwide. Heat is generated by fossil fuels such as natural gas and propane, and by electricity, which in turn relies on fossil fuels. Of the fossil fuels burned for electricity, coal is by far the most prevalent, producing 40 percent of the world's electricity, followed by natural gas, which produces 21 percent. Coal also has more impact on global warming than natural gas because it emits twice as much carbon dioxide per unit of energy. In the United States, coal is responsible for nearly one-third of the carbon dioxide emissions.

If coal is a leading greenhouse gas emitter, why is it even used for electricity? Coal has a distinct advantage: it's cheap, because it's plentiful. However, as natural gas becomes more available in the United States, it is pricing out coal. Beginning in around 2000, new technologies, such as hydraulic fracking (producing artificial fractures in rocks so that gas can be taken out) have led to a boom in natural gas. U.S. carbon emissions declined overall from 2007 to 2012 due in part to the switch from coal to natural gas for power. Some scientists believe that natural gas, a lower greenhouse gas emitter than coal, should be used until greener technologies are in place. But natural gas is not without controversy. Some mismanaged projects have allowed fracturing fluids to seep into area soil and water supplies, posing health hazards to people and animals. The storage of waste water in the course of fracking has also been shown to cause earthquakes in some cases. And leaky natural gas equipment can release another greenhouse gas — methane — into the atmosphere.

In addition to competition from natural gas, coal is facing friction from the EPA. The EPA is investigating whether coal-fired power plants are complying with the Clean Air Act, a federal law that prohibits companies from polluting the air. The EPA is also bringing carbon dioxide emissions under the Clean Air umbrella, meaning that coal companies will no longer be able to freely spew greenhouse gases into the air. Redesigning plants to conform to these rules will be costly. Elsewhere, renewable resources are already taking the place of coal. Deutche Bank said in 2013 that coal use peaked in the European Union in 2012, and would decline as wind, solar, and hydro energy were added to power grids.

However, nations like China and India are using more coal

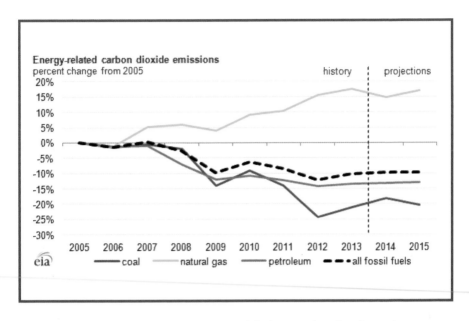

Energy-related carbon dioxide emissions
percent change from 2005

The use of natural gas rose from 2007–12, while the use of coal and petroleum declined. Because natural gas emits less carbon dioxide than the other two, the overall carbon dioxide emissions declined, as shown by the dotted line.

than ever. A Peabody Energy study estimated that world demand would grow from 8.7 billion tons (7.9 billion metric tons) in 2012 to 9.8 billion tons (8.9 billion metric tons) in 2016, and that China would account for much of that demand. China, now the leading producer and consumer of coal, had 620 coal-fired plants operating in 2012, and was expected to add 160 more by 2016.[13] China favors coal for the same reason the United States does: it's cheap. And for China, it's fueled an industrial revolution that has lifted 680 million people out of poverty. But it's also causing a serious pollution problem.

In Northern China, smog has forced airports to shut down due to decreased visibility and schools to close due to the dangerous air. Journalists have dubbed such days "airmageddon" and "airpocalypse." On these days, children aren't allowed to play outside at all, and those with respiratory diseases like asthma often require hospital visits. The World Health Organization says that the air is safe to breathe when particulate matter from pollution is 25 micrograms per cubic meter or less. In Harbin, a large Chinese city, readings have exceeded 600. This severe pollution caused 1.2 million premature deaths in China in 2010 alone.[14] Growing unrest among citizens has led the Chinese government to require provinces to reduce pollution by 5 to 25 percent by reducing the use of coal, eliminating outdated industrial systems, and limiting vehicle pollution. A persistent crackdown on pollution may have the added effect of reducing greenhouse gas emissions.

Meanwhile, 1.2 billion people—mainly in Asia and sub-Saharan Africa—still have no access to modern energy. People burn wood, coal, dung, or crop waste in stoves or open fires to cook and heat their homes. This creates indoor air pollution that kills 3.5 million people each year.[15] The cruel irony is that these same people, whose impoverished way of life means that they've contributed very little to global warming, will bear the brunt of climate change as drought ravishes Africa and rising sea levels flood parts of Asia.

Coal has fueled an industrial revolution in China, creating dangerous air pollution levels in cities such as Shanghai.

TRANSPORTATION AND OIL

In the United States, transportation is second to electricity as the leading greenhouse gas source (it is fifth worldwide). Americans own a whopping 660 vehicles per one thousand people.[16] And there are more air travelers than ever—more than seven hundred million per year now, and more than one billion expected by 2030.[17] As a result, the demand for oil is 18.8 million barrels per day in the United States, a large chunk of the 89-million-barrel demand worldwide. (One barrel is 42 gallons or 159 liters.)

While stricter fuel economy standards are expected to lower demand for oil in America and other developed nations, the increase in cars and second cars driven by the growing middle class in developing nations like China, India, and Russia will increase demand there. In 2000, there were four cars per one thousand people worldwide. By 2010, that had grown to forty per one thousand people, and by 2035 it will

A traffic jam in Old Delhi, India, consists of cars, rickshaws, and pedestrians. As the middle class grows in India, there are more cars on the road. Worldwide, 1.7 billion vehicles are expected to be in use by 2035, making alternative fuels essential to curbing the world's oil consumption.

The demand for oil has led to more offshore drilling, including deep-water drilling for oil that was once unattainable.

balloon to 310 per one thousand people, for a total of 1.7 billion cars on the road. Whether those vehicles will be powered by oil or a lower-emission fuel remains to be seen.

Oil has always been a finite resource. However, new technologies have allowed once-unattainable oil to be drilled, so that lately the supply of oil has seemed bottomless. Unfortunately, this newfound oil is sometimes even dirtier than regular oil. Canada is the top exporter to the United States, but the oil now being mined from the Oil Sand Reserve of Northern Alberta is the consistency of molasses. For this reason, it requires more energy to procure, process, and transport. In addition, to access this oil, forest must be cleared and tons of peat and dirt removed. Each barrel of this type of once-unattainable oil emits as much as three times the greenhouse gases as other oil.

INDUSTRY

Though transportation is the second leading greenhouse gas emitter in America, industry comes in second worldwide. Industry emissions come from burning fossil fuels for energy to make things. Top greenhouse gas emitting industries include iron, steel, aluminum, machine manufacturing, paper, food and tobacco, chemicals, oil and gas, coal, and cement. Greenhouse gases can also be emitted through the chemical reactions required to convert raw materials to products. One such reaction occurs during the manufacture of cement. Cement is made from limestone. Limestone, also called calcium carbonate, is composed of shells and corals, which contain carbon. When calcium carbonate is converted to lime for concrete, carbon dioxide is released. This process also requires intense heat, and thus energy, which requires the burning of fossil fuels. For these reasons, cement is a top industrial greenhouse gas emitter.

FORESTRY

After industry, forestry is responsible for the most greenhouse gas emissions throughout the world. Tropical rainforests are particularly susceptible to deforestation. They are cleared first for roads and lumber, and then for farms. Historically, Brazil has led the world in deforestation. In 2004, 10,425 square miles (27,000 square kilometers) of forest was cleared.[18] Since then, the country has made strides in reducing deforestation, but the problem is widespread in South America, Southeast Asia, and Africa. Government policies can help reduce deforestation, but poverty also plays a role. Much of the forest land being cleared is by people who will use the land for farms to feed their families.

AGRICULTURE

Farms throughout the world are the fourth leading cause of greenhouse gas emissions. Here, greenhouse gas emissions come from a variety of sources. Tilling the land releases carbon dioxide held in the soil. Manure and gas from grazing animals emit methane. Fertilizer contributes to emissions of the potent greenhouse gas nitrous oxide. To reduce emissions, farmers have been employing greener methods, such as no-till farming—planting crops without turning over the soil, storing manure for reuse as fuel, and grazing cattle on prairie grasses (which store carbon dioxide in their roots). Scientists have also been looking at ways to reduce agricultural emissions. For instance, feeding cattle genetically engineered grass that is easier to digest could reduce the methane in the animals' gas. (See sidebar, The Skeptics on the Other Side: GMOs.)

THE FORECAST FOR EMISSIONS

While reducing emissions from deforestation and agriculture is important, the majority of greenhouse gas emissions come

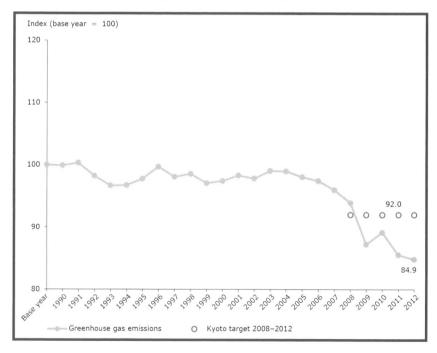

The original 15 European Union countries together have cut their greenhouse gas emissions to 84.9 percent of (or 15.1 percent below) 1990 levels. The current 28 EU countries have made even deeper cuts.

from burning fossil fuels. The future of fossil fuels in large part will determine the future of global warming. Carbon dioxide emissions from power generation in the United States rose steadily from 1990 to 2007, but have since fallen to 10 percent below 2005 levels. Much of that is due to higher fuel standards, the shift from coal to natural gas, and increased use of renewables like hydropower and wind. Other developed nations have made deeper cuts. The EU's emissions are 18 percent below their 1990 levels.

Elsewhere, though, emissions are still on the rise, particularly in developing nations with rapidly growing economies. With the world's current reliance on fossil fuels, these growing economies will mean growing emissions. The developing world is becoming more like America, and Americans consume a lot of energy. The world population is projected to reach 9.6 billion by 2050, but if the world starts to live as Americans do right now, it would be like the population had grown to seventy-two billion in terms of energy consumption.[19]

Will we continue on our path of high energy consumption? Or will we become more efficient and switch to greener energy? The answer to those questions will determine just how hot—and how bad—things will get.

BE THE CHANGE

WHAT: Reduce industry emissions.

HOW: Buy used furniture, accessories, clothing, and more.

WHY: Worldwide, industry is the second largest greenhouse gas contributor. By reducing the amount of new goods you buy, you'll help decrease the demand for them and ultimately cut back on these emissions.

WHAT ELSE: If you do buy new furniture or other wood products, avoid wood obtained by destroying forests. The Forest Stewardship Council ensures that wood comes from forests or plantations where trees are replanted and endangered species are protected. This wood bears an **FSC-certified label**.

Skeptics on the Other Side: GMOs

Genetically engineered crops are created in a lab. Scientists take a plant with a desirable trait. In the case of genetically engineered grass for cattle, for instance, the desired trait is digestibility. They extract the gene from the plant that makes it digestible. Then they insert the gene into the plant they are trying to change, such as grass that will be fed to cows. When the genetically engineered grass grows, scientists crossbreed it with hardy specimens of grass (grass that does not die easily). They harvest the seeds, and those seeds are then planted by farmers. The new crop of grass is now more easily digestible, and the cows that eat it emit less methane in their gas.

More easily digested grass is just one example of a genetically engineered plant. In the United States, genetically engineered soybeans, corn, and canola are ubiquitous. Walk down your supermarket aisle, and 60 percent of the processed foods you see, from pancake mix to ice cream, contain these genetically engineered ingredients.

You likely have also heard about genetically engineered crops in the news or through social media. Often referred to as GMOs (genetically modified organisms), they are quite controversial. Consumer watch groups have said they are unhealthy and have demanded that companies label genetically engineered foods as a warning to consumers. But just as the scientific position is that global warming is real, the scientific consensus is that genetically engineered crops are safe to eat and safe for the environment. In fact, scientists say genetic engineering is really not very different from what farm-

ers have been doing for thousands of years. In the past, they would select seeds from the hardiest plants to plant the next year. They would also crossbreed two plants to create one that had desirable traits from both. Genetic engineering is simply a more efficient way of doing this.

Interestingly, many people who side with scientists on the topic of global warming do not accept the scientific viewpoint on GMOs. So news stories of GMOs causing cancer, for instance, have spread throughout media outlets, even though such studies have later been retracted. You can find scientists who question the safety of GMOs, just as you can find those who question the validity of global warming. But the major scientific bodies, including the U.S. National Academy of Sciences and the American Medical Association, say that GMOs are safe.

Note that I have no bias toward GMOs, only a bias toward science, if you would call that "bias." (To me being biased toward science, with its rigorous demands for testing and accuracy, is essentially being biased toward the truth.) The point of this sidebar is to show that we can't pick and choose scientific facts based on gut reactions or political leanings. Scientific facts remain true whether we believe in them or not. It's what we choose to do with the information that matters. In the case of genetically engineered crops, they could help reduce greenhouse gas emissions, as seen in the example of genetically engineered grass. They could also help to ease the burden of climate change. For instance, scientists are engineering crops to withstand droughts brought about by global warming. These would help farmers—and all of us—to cope with the drier days ahead.

PART FOUR
NATURE AND
HUMAN NATURE

CHAPTER 10
NATURE'S FURY:
HOW HOT? HOW BAD?

WHILE SOME POLITICIANS AND PUNDITS question whether global warming is happening, in the scientific community, the questions are: How hot will it get, and how bad will the fallout be? The answers to these questions are important for two main reasons. First, they allow countries to set goals for cutting emissions in order to avoid catastrophic climate change. (Of course, politicians must first listen to the scientists and agree to take action.) Then, they allow governments to prepare for the effects of global warming that are most likely going to happen.

Scientists predict climate change by entering possible future greenhouse gas levels into climate models. The problem is that future greenhouse gas levels depend on something very unpredictable: people. So scientists have set up various scenarios based on how we may respond to the global warming crisis. Some scenarios assume that a few decades from now we will have reduced greenhouse gas emissions, others that we will have kept emissions level, and still others that we will have allowed them to rise. Scientists plug in the various greenhouse gas levels to the climate models and observe what happens to the climate. The results are tested against historical and current climate data.

Based on the various scenarios, the 2013 IPCC report estimates that carbon dioxide emissions will rise to between 421 and 936 parts per million by 2100, and the increase in temperature from late-nineteenth-century levels will range from 1.8 degrees F (1 degree C) to greater than 7.2 degrees F (4 degrees C). Sea level would rise 0.85–3.2 feet (0.26–0.98 meters) above 1986–2005 levels. Let's look at how bad things could get based on these figures.

SEA LEVEL RISE

Rising sea level could displace millions of people, many of whom are already poor and have nowhere to go. We've seen that rising sea level is already inundating island nations in the Pacific. An additional rise of 1.6 feet (0.5 meters) would inundate low-lying, heavily populated areas such as Alexandria, Egypt; Venice, Italy; New Orleans; and the nations of Bangladesh and the Netherlands. A 3-foot (1-meter) rise would flood the cities of New York, Miami, Tokyo, Bangkok, and Shanghai and could displace one hundred million people.

Asia will probably be the continent hardest hit by rising sea level. Vietnam would see ten million people displaced,

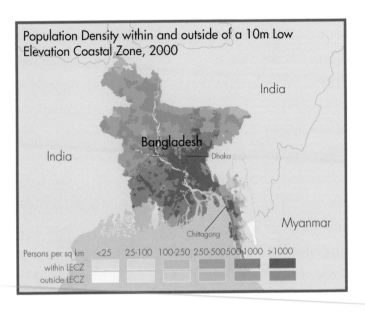

Population Density within and outside of a 10m Low Elevation Coastal Zone, 2000

India

Bangladesh

India

Dhaka

Myanmar

Chittagong

Persons per sq km: <25 | 25-100 | 100-250 | 250-500 | 500-1000 | >1000
within LECZ
outside LECZ

A 1-meter rise in sea level would displace 15–20 million people in Bangladesh alone. This would drive people who are already poor into refugee camps, where crowded quarters have historically led to hunger and disease. This is one reason why global warming could cause the biggest humanitarian crisis of our time.

Malaysia another ten million, and the list goes on. In the book *Six Degrees*, the author Mark Lynas describes what would happen in Bangladesh should sea level rise by 3 feet (1 meter). With an average annual income of $1,440, Bangladesh is among the world's poorest countries. A 3-foot rise in sea level would uproot fifteen to twenty million of its people. They would be sent to refugee camps, where food is short and disease runs rampant. However, finding a place for refugee camps would be difficult in the already crowded nation. (Bangladesh has 1,100 people per square kilometer, compared to 33 per square kilometer in the United States.) And neighboring India likely wouldn't be able to handle refugees, as it would be facing its own flood crisis. East Africa, Egypt, Latin America, and coastal cities around the world would have global warming refugees needing homes, and that's just with a 3-foot rise.

The past indicates that sea level will rise higher than that. About 125,000 years ago, when the global temperature was just 3.6 degrees F (2 degrees C) higher than today, the sea level was 16.5–33 feet (5–10 meters) higher.[20] For this reason, the IPCC predicts that if the global temperature rises 1.8–7 degrees F (1–4 degrees C), the Greenland ice sheet will likely melt, not immediately, but over the course of one thousand or more years. If the West Antarctic ice sheet contributed an additional 10 feet (3 meters), 25 percent of the world population would be displaced.[21]

The sea will not rise gradually, like a bathtub being filled, but rather in surges that occur during storms. The warmer atmosphere will hold more moisture, causing intense storms to occur more frequently. Cities will be inundated so many times that eventually it will be unfeasible to rebuild. Coastal farmland, meanwhile, will become contaminated with salt water. Farther inland, people will face worsening droughts.

DROUGHT

The 2013 IPCC report states that in general, wet climates will become wetter, and dry climates, drier. That means that the

Mediterranean, south and northwest Africa, and the southwest United States will likely endure droughts. Africa will be hit hard, as one-third of the population lives in drought-prone areas. History shows that drought can lead not only to famine, but also to war.

In *Overheated: The Human Cost of Climate Change,* Andrew Guzman describes how the genocide in Sudan was sparked by a drought that may have been the result of global warming. Arab herdsmen had been allowed by non-Arabs known as the Fur to use their wells and a portion of their crops to feed and water the herdsmen's animals. But decreased rainfall in Darfur (a region of Sudan) beginning in the early 1980s made water scarce on these farms. Feeling that they had no water or crops to spare, the Fur fenced off their lands and didn't allow the nomads in. Violence broke out. The mostly Arab government sided with Arab groups, which in turn caused the farmers to rebel in 2003. The rebellion was quashed violently: two hundred thousand of the Fur were killed by the Sudanese government. Millions were displaced, and many continue to live in refugee camps.

Food and water shortages are a recipe for disaster. With global warming, food shortages would occur first in dry regions and the tropics, where food productivity will decrease if the local temperature rises just 1.8–3.6 degrees F (1 or 2 degrees C).[22] Elsewhere, food production will increase with a small amount of warming. But after the world is 2.7–6.3 degrees F (1.5–3.5 degrees C) warmer than it was in the late nineteenth century, food production will decrease worldwide. Canada and Russia may enjoy longer growing seasons, and fertile land may open up in the Arctic as the glaciers melt. But food production in the north will not make up for the agricultural woes happening elsewhere. And while it may seem that excess carbon dioxide would be a boon to plants, scien-

This notice was posted during a drought in Queensland, Australia. Global warming has already been the culprit of droughts around the world. In the future, scientists expect that the U.S. Southwest will endure chronic drought conditions.

tists believe the atmospheric change will favor leafy, weed-like vines over food crops.

The United States would face its own crisis with a worsening drought in the Southwest. Climate models show that drying is already under way because of global warming, and that the new climate may come to resemble the Dust Bowl of the 1930s.[23] During the Dust Bowl, a nearly decade-long drought, coupled with unsustainable farming methods, caused the soil to turn to dust and be swept up into dust storms. These storms buried farms in Oklahoma, Texas, New Mexico, and Colorado in dust, driving people from their homes.

VANISHING GLACIERS

Water shortages will also be caused by shrinking mountain glaciers. One-sixth of the world's population relies on glaciers for water.[24] These glaciers melt partially in the spring, and the meltwater runs downstream to be used for irrigation and power. In the winter, the glaciers are replenished by snowfall. Now the glaciers are melting entirely. For instance, the glacier on Chacaltaya Mountain formerly supplied water to much of Bolivia. It had melted completely by 2009. Today, glaciers in the Hindu Kush, Karakoram, and Himalayan mountain ranges provide water to Southeast Asia—where a quarter of the world's people live. As the climate warms, these

Shrinking glaciers will lead to water shortages, as people around the world rely on glacial meltwater to irrigate their crops in the spring.

glaciers, too, are melting, contributing to the rising sea level rather than being available to irrigate farms and power cities.

FROM BAD TO WORSE

At the risk of sounding like a Debbie Downer, things could get even worse. If carbon dioxide exceeds 936 parts per million, the IPCC predicts that the temperature could rise 7.2 degrees F (4 degrees C) or higher above late-nineteenth-century lev-

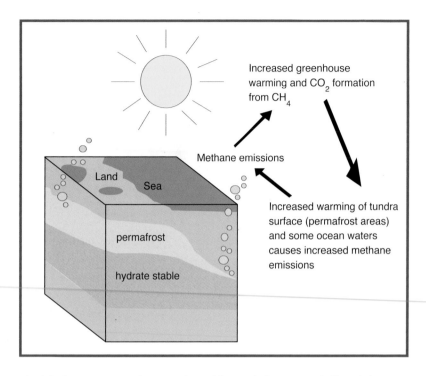

Increased greenhouse warming and CO_2 formation from CH_4

Methane emissions

Increased warming of tundra surface (permafrost areas) and some ocean waters causes increased methane emissions

Land

Sea

permafrost

hydrate stable

With global warming, methane ice buried beneath the ocean shelf and slope are believed to be melting. As a result, scientists think methane from the ocean shelf is being released into the atmosphere. Methane is a powerful greenhouse gas.

els. While any rise in temperature will cause big problems, a 7.2-degree-F rise could cause runaway global warming. That is, positive feedback would become so powerful that our greenhouse gas emissions would be only part of the problem causing global warming. The rest would be caused by factors that were beyond our control.

We've talked about the decrease in the sun's reflection as snow and ice melts, but there are other positive feedback

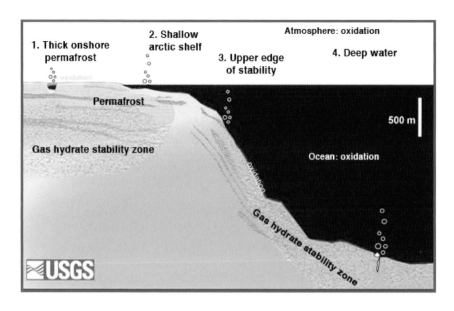

This map shows the four sectors in which methane ice is buried. In sector 1, methane ice will likely melt only after thousands of years of warming. The methane ice in sector 2, which is thought to make up 1 percent of the methane ice in the world, is probably already melting and being released into the atmosphere. Scientists think methane ice is also melting in sector 3, but that it is remaining in the ocean rather than being released into the atmosphere. Ninety-five percent of the world's methane ice exists in sector 4, which isn't likely to melt even after thousands of years of warming.

factors too. Warming oceans store less carbon dioxide, causing the atmosphere to absorb more. In a process known as carbon cycle feedback, warming soil causes bacteria to break down organic matter faster, so that the soil releases rather than stores carbon dioxide. And as Arctic permafrost melts, it releases carbon dioxide too.

A wildcard possibility in all of this is the release of methane by the melting of methane ice. Today, methane ice can be found deep in the permafrost of the Arctic, deep in the sea floor, and along the ocean slope. Most of this methane ice is stable. That is, one thousand years of warming would not likely lead to melting. The methane on the ocean slope is the exception. It represents only a small portion of the methane ice in the world, but is the most susceptible to melting after one hundred years of warming. Scientists are unsure how much methane would be released should this ocean slope ice melt. They are studying it because of the role methane ice may have played in past extreme-warming events.

Should runaway global warming cause the eventual melting of both polar ice caps, it would result in a 262-foot (80-meter) rise in sea level. America would begin to look like a map of Panem from *The Hunger Games*, with Florida, Louisiana, and much of the Gulf Coast and Eastern Seaboard underwater. Worldwide, the number of climate-change refugees would be staggering, and water and food shortages would be widespread. The point of this is not to cause panic, but to show that we should never throw our hands up and say, "If global warming is already happening, there's no sense fighting it now." It is worth making an effort to stop global warming at every degree. Because if global warming can be limited to one degree, that's better than two, two is better than three, and three is definitely better than four.

BE THE CHANGE

WHAT: Reduce industry emissions.

HOW: Fix items that are broken or torn rather than buying new ones.

WHY: In past generations, things were repaired rather than thrown away in order to save money. Because goods are relatively cheaper now, this has become a lost art. But we pay a price for our disposable lifestyle: increased greenhouse gas emissions from making and transporting new products. Learn to sew on a button, iron on a patch, or artfully duct tape a broken laundry basket, and you'll reduce industry greenhouse emissions, save money, and feel a sense of pride for knowing how to do this.

WHAT ELSE: Make things from what you have on hand rather than buying them. An old T-shirt can be turned into a dress, laundry detergent containers can be turned into storage buckets, tires can be made into play sets, and there are many other ideas on social media sites.

Some scientists believe that the Greenland ice sheet could collapse not in one thousand years, but in one hundred. In the article "Can We Defuse the Global Warming Time Bomb?" the former NASA climatologist James Hansen says that not only are rising sea levels the biggest global warming concern, but that the rate at which the Greenland ice sheet will melt is underestimated. He predicts that with a 1.8-degree-F (1-degree-C) rise in global temperature, large portions of the ice sheet could melt by the end of this century. He cites several factors: Rising sea level will break up the sea ice that protects the land ice from ocean water. When the ocean water floods parts of the ice sheet, it will melt the ice. As the ice breaks up, it will

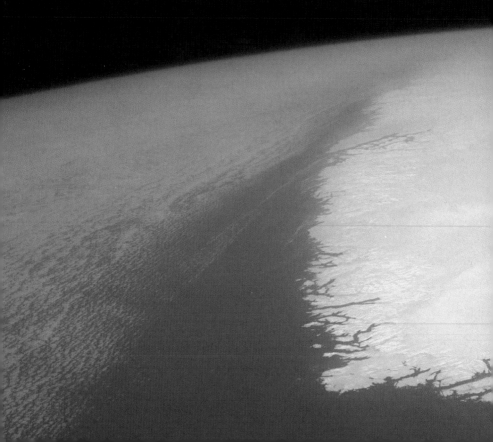

ment faster, as broken ice melts faster than solid ice. Warming rain will increase and darken the ice, decreasing its ability to reflect sunlight.

For further evidence, Hansen looks to the Eemian (an interglacial period during the last ice age), when the temperature was 1.8 degrees F (1 degree C) warmer than in the mid-1900s, and sea level was 16–20 feet (5–6 meters) higher. On the positive side, he thinks that we can prevent global temperature from rising more than 1.8 degrees F by capturing carbon at new coal-fired power plants, reducing black-carbon air pollution, and making a dramatic change in fuel efficiency standards.

CHAPTER 11
SO SHOULD I BE WORRIED?

HAVING READ THIS FAR, YOU know that we should all be worried about global warming. So why *aren't* people more worried? Why isn't there more of an outcry? Why isn't more being done? To understand this, scientists have begun studying not only global warming, but the psychology of global warming.

Global warming is a rare case where scientific experts are more anxious than laypersons.[25] If you look at other scientific issues, such as GMOs, non-scientists tend to be more worried than scientists. With global warming, however, the opposite is true. Scientists are saying loud and clear that global warming is happening, and that it is causing economic and health problems for people around the world. But non-scientists don't seem to have a sense of urgency about this.

Many people simply aren't hearing the message. A 2013 Gallup poll found that only 52 percent of Republicans and 74 percent of Democrats think that most scientists believe that global warming is happening. Further, just 39 percent of

Republicans and 78 percent of Democrats believe that global warming is mainly caused by human factors. Finally, only 75 percent of Democrats and 40 percent of Republicans are worried about global warming.

What accounts for such a chill reaction to global warming? In an article in the journal *Nature Climate Change,* "Climate Change and Moral Judgment," the scientists Ezra Markowitz and Azim Shariff state that "human moral judgment is not equipped to view climate change as a moral imperative." They give six reasons:

> **Complexity:** Global warming requires complex intellectual thought, and this type of thinking doesn't lead to the sort of gut reaction that causes people to take action.
>
> **Unintentional nature of the problem:** Global warming is the unintended consequence of using energy, and inadvertent wrongs are not viewed to be as egregious as intentional ones.
>
> **Guilt:** People who do feel guilty about contributing to global warming may downplay their actions in order to feel better about themselves.
>
> **Optimism:** We tend to interpret uncertainty overly optimistically, and many people believe that the science of global warming is more uncertain than it really is.
>
> **Politics:** We follow the teachings of our political groups in order to feel part of those groups. The Republican

Party line has been that global warming does not exist, or if it does, is not caused primarily by human activity, or even if it is, is not cause for concern. In other words, that there is no problem, or at least no solution.

It's in the future and far away: We feel less obliged to help faraway or future people. In the same Gallup poll cited above, only 54 percent of people said they believe that global warming is happening right now.

But blaming human nature only goes so far. Other countries have made sweeping changes to reduce emissions, and their people have the same human nature that Americans have. What makes us different? Perhaps Americans are reluctant to act because we do not yet feel vulnerable. In China and India, where flooding and water shortages have led people to feel vulnerable to climate change, more than 70 percent of those surveyed by Pew Research were willing to pay more for energy in order to address climate change. Only 38 percent of U.S. respondents said that they would pay more. Will Americans change their minds in the wake of natural disasters?

After Hurricanes Irene and Sandy, and the 2011 Halloween blizzard, nearly two-thirds of New Jerseyans thought climate change was to blame, according to a *Rutgers-Eagleton* poll. Viewpoints still varied along party lines, with only 33 percent of Republicans believing this. Nearly three-fourths of those who blamed storms on climate change said the storms made them more likely to believe climate change is real. Of course, it would be much better if people felt a sense of urgency before such natural disasters became commonplace.

It may be that people need more education. In the study World Wide Views on Global Warming, 4,400 people in thirty-eight countries were given a day of education about global warming. Afterward, 90 percent of people worldwide and 95 percent of people in the United States said they were very or fairly concerned. The study said that to raise awareness about global warming, the media should talk more on the issue without giving climate skeptics equal billing with mainstream scientists.

Now, let's look at how individual behavior has changed in the past. You probably buckle up as soon as you get into a car. But wearing a seat belt used to be a rarity. I grew up in the 1980s and don't remember ever wearing a seat belt. That was common; in 1984, U.S. seat belt use was just 14 percent, according to the National Highway Traffic Safety Administration. Only when I started high school in the 1990s did I begin to hear the phrase "Buckle up." Since then, seat belt use across America has risen to 85 percent. So how did this happen? Did all Americans suddenly see the light—that seat belts save lives? It wasn't that simple.

Even the seemingly individual choice of buckling up actually came about through laws and awareness campaigns. Starting in 1974, all vehicles were required to have seat belts. The trick was to get people to wear them. In 1984, New York was the first state to enact a seat belt law. Other states

This sign, posted in the carpool line of a grade school, never would have existed prior to the mid-1980s, because hardly anyone back then wore seat belts. When New York enacted a seat belt law in 1984, only 14 percent of people in that state wore seat belts. Today, seat belt use is 90 percent in New York, and even higher in some states.

followed suit and also launched advertising campaigns to inform people of the new laws and about how seat belts save lives. As a result, seat belt use increased dramatically—from 14 to 42 percent between 1984 and 1987 alone. It has risen steadily ever since. States with the highest seat belt use rates have laws that allow police officers to pull people over solely for not wearing seat belts. (In other states, people are ticketed for not wearing seat belts only if they have already been pulled over for another reason.) The seemingly individual decision to wear a seat belt is rooted in government intervention.

This example is worth noting because it's often said that

if people demand change—if they demand a better climate policy, for instance—the government will change. But most people weren't demanding that their governments enact seat belt laws. Indeed, if individuals had wanted to wear seat belts, they could have. But state governments thought that enacting seat belt laws to save lives was the right thing to do.

Global warming is different from seat belt use in that it is the result not only of individual decisions but also of decisions made by businesses, organizations, and governments. So we need to look at how some bigger changes—especially those pertaining to the environment—have happened in the past. (Spoiler alert: the government has taken action.)

> **Sewer systems.** In the 1800s, people in industrialized cities throughout the world were surrounded by their own sewage. In Edinburgh, Scotland, residents threw their sewage out the window. In London, sewage flowed into the River Thames, and people then drank the untreated water. In city slums everywhere, sewage was contained in open cesspools that leaked into wells. Not only did this create a disgusting smell, it also led to the spread of disease. Cholera epidemics swept the world from the 1830s to the 1860s. In London alone, the disease killed nearly forty thousand people. At first, people thought the disease spread through the air. However, London doctor John Snow was able to prove that it spread through contaminated drinking water. In light of this public health

problem, local governments revamped their cities to include sewer systems. In London, for instance, Parliament sanctioned new sewers in 1865.

Water pollution. In the 1970s, America had a water pollution problem. Thirty percent of drinking water contained chemicals exceeding health standards. With untreated sewage being pumped into the nation's waterways, two-thirds of U.S. lakes, rivers, and coastal areas were unsafe for swimming or fishing. In 1972, the U.S. government enacted the Clean Water Act, cracking down on industrial pollution. It demanded that by 1985, zero pollution would be released into navigable waters. Though court rulings have sometimes weakened the Act, it has still managed to keep billions of pounds of pollution out of U.S. waters.[26]

Chlorofluorocarbons. These chemicals were developed in the 1930s and used as coolants in refrigerators and air conditioners, in the manufacture of Styrofoam, and in aerosol sprays such as hairspray. Then scientists in the 1970s theorized that such chemicals would be unstable in the upper atmosphere, converting ozone (O_3) into oxygen (O_2), thus depleting the ozone. Scientists working in Antarctica confirmed the theory in 1985. An image broadcast on the TV news of a giant hole in the ozone led to public outcry. As a result, chlorofluorocarbons were banned internationally at the 1989 Montreal Protocol. For their work in discovering ozone depletion,

Paul Crutzen, Mario Molina, and F. Sherwood Rowland received the 1985 Nobel Prize for chemistry.

Seat belt laws preceded seat belt use. The Clean Water Act preceded pollution reduction. And the Montreal Protocol preceded the end of chlorofluorocarbons. In all these cases, the government acted. So perhaps we are putting the cart before the horse in expecting individuals to make changes that realistically require government action. Where changes can be made easily, people *have* changed—using LED or fluorescent light bulbs even when incandescent lights were still on the market, buying Energy Star products, and recycling. But many changes that would reduce greenhouse gas emissions are not easily adoptable. Most cars are powered by gasoline,

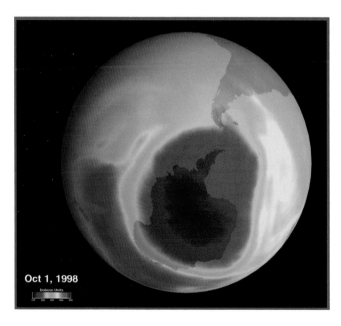

Oct 1, 1998

An image of a hole in the ozone caused by chlorofluorocarbons propelled people into action, and the chemicals were banned internationally in 1989.

most homes are powered by fossil fuels, and many communities are so spread out that walking everywhere is impractical. As it is, asking people to make sweeping changes in their energy consumption is a little like telling people to buckle up before cars were manufactured to have seat belts. Sure, they could install their own seat belts, and a few rugged individuals would, but most people wouldn't.

It would be wonderful if we lived in a world where everyone went out of their way to do the right and prudent thing in every area of their lives, but that is not the reality. Somebody probably mentioned to me growing up that seat belts saved lives, and I wish I could say that that's when I started wearing one, but the truth is, I didn't until the laws and public service campaigns changed the habits of everyone, including me.

Looking beyond environmental issues, the government has acted in important ways even when individuals didn't. Congress has passed laws to abolish slavery, reform labor, and enact Civil Rights. Like global warming, these issues were controversial in their day. But eventually Congress acted to protect the rights of U.S. citizens to life, liberty, and the pursuit of happiness. Perhaps the effects of global warming are not felt acutely enough yet for people to demand reform. But by the time they are, much of the damage will be done. Droughts, wildfires, storms, and floods will have created a global health crisis that encompasses the United States. With or without a public outcry, the U.S. government has the responsibility to act now to prevent such a crisis. With one of only two major political parties denying anthropogenic global warming, that will be difficult.

And the question remains, how did a scientific fact become a matter of political debate at all?

BE THE CHANGE

WHAT: *Reduce industry emissions.*

HOW: *Don't buy overpackaged items.*

WHY: *Not only does packaging clog landfills when it's not recycled, but the manufacture of packaging requires energy. In the grocery store, buy fresh fruits and vegetables—which have natural packaging in the form of their skins—and put them in a reusable bag. If you see something with ridiculous overpackaging, such as oranges peeled and placed in plastic containers, single-serving cereal boxes, or a gadget package that takes up more space than the gadget itself, don't buy it.*

WHAT ELSE: *Forgo plastic bags. Like all other packaging, these require energy to make, and though recyclable, they're not always collected by municipal recycling trucks. Bring your own reusable bag to the store instead.*

CHAPTER 12
THE POLITICS OF
GLOBAL WARMING

GLOBAL WARMING WASN'T ALWAYS POLITICALLY polarizing. In 1992, Republican George H. W. Bush joined nearly
two hundred other world leaders in signing the United Nations Framework Convention on Climate Change document
attributing climate change to human activity and making a
goal of avoiding dangerous anthropogenic interference by re-
turning greenhouse gas emissions to 1990 levels. Emissions
continued to rise worldwide, leading to meetings in Berlin
in 1995, Geneva in 1996, and Kyoto in 1997. In Kyoto, an
addendum called the Kyoto Protocol was added to the document. The addendum stated the same goal but specified what
each nation would do to reach that goal. For the European
Union, it was to reduce greenhouse gas emissions to 8 percent
below 1990 levels, and for the United States, 7 percent.

By now, Democrat Bill Clinton was in office, and both
Democrats and Republicans in Congress were against the
Kyoto Protocol. Both sides objected to the fact that develop-

ing nations would not be required to meet emissions goals. They had a point. Even if the United States and every other signing country had met its Kyoto obligation, emissions would have climbed worldwide because of the growing emissions in developing countries. At the same time, there was a reason for leaving the developing nations out of the emissions requirement. It would allow them to grow their economies—thus reducing poverty—by using cheap fossil fuels for energy. At any rate, the Senate unanimously voted against ratifying the protocol.

During the 2000 presidential campaign, both Democratic candidate Al Gore and Republican candidate George W. Bush promised to limit greenhouse gas emissions. But once elected, Bush did an about-face, saying that the science of climate change was uncertain, that limiting carbon emissions would raise energy prices, and that his administration would not regulate emissions after all. That's when global warming became a politically polarizing issue.

Global warming denial picked up speed. In 2005, the Republican senator James Inhofe gave a speech on the Senate floor, denying that global warming was caused by people. He cited Michael Crichton, the author of *Jurassic Park* and other science fiction titles, as a source. Frank Luntz, a political consultant, wrote a strategy memo to Republicans in Congress urging them to say that scientists were still on the fence about global warming. The memo stated, "Voters believe that there is no consensus about global warming in the scientific community. Should the public come to believe that specific issues are settled, their views about global warming will change accordingly."[27]

What's behind the skepticism and denial? It's helpful to look at who is funding it. Disbelief in global warming isn't something people happen to have (like how some people believe in ghosts). Rather it's based on information that has been spread by groups whose purpose is to create those doubts. And these groups are funded by fossil fuel companies. According to the Union of Concerned Scientists, which promotes scientific accuracy in government policies, one such group includes the Heartland Institute, which is funded by Exxon Mobil and Koch Industries (a coal company). Scientists working for the Heartland Institute offer expert opinions to news outlets and government panels that call into question the science of global warming. Interestingly, the Heartland Institute has also offered expert opinions on tobacco, claiming that secondhand smoke does not cause lung cancer. You would be hard-pressed to find a doctor who supported that claim. Other such groups—funded by coal, oil, and gas—include Americans for Prosperity, American Legislative Exchange Council, and Beacon Hill Institute at Suffolk University.

These groups, along with the oil, coal, and gas companies who bankroll them, also make campaign contributions to politicians. James Inhofe's top campaign contributors have included Americans for Prosperity. During President George

W. Bush's term, he received more money from the oil and gas industries than any other president.[28] It would stand to reason that such contributions would affect the viewpoints of politicians. And because people tend to subscribe to the viewpoint of their political party, global warming skepticism spread among Republican voters, too.

It's important to note that climate-change skepticism isn't neatly divided along party lines. Only 70 percent of Republican members of Congress actually deny anthropogenic global warming, according to the *Guardian*. Some Republicans have encouraged colleagues to move past the scientific debate and start discussing Republican-minded policies that will address global warming. Likewise, voters don't fall into neat categories. In a 2012 Gallup Poll, 26 percent of Democrats said that they believed there was no scientific consensus about global warming. However, it's undeniable that global warming skepticism among some Republicans has created gridlock for politicians trying to address climate change.

In 2006, with Al Gore's Oscar-winning documentary *An Inconvenient Truth*, the tide seemed to turn. Everybody was talking about going green, and both Democrat and Republican presidential candidates in 2008 pledged to cut carbon emissions. But global warming was dealt several blows in the years to follow. New domestic oil and natural gas sources made renewable energy less popular. The housing market collapsed, plunging the nation into a recession and shifting the public's focus from global warming to unemployment and home foreclosures. A scandal known as Climategate also took a toll.

At the Climatic Research Unit of the University of Anglia, the server was hacked and about one thousand emails regarding climate-change data were leaked. Quotes taken from the emails were said to indicate that the climate scientists were trying to hide data from critics. An Associated Press investigation of the emails found that while data wasn't shared as freely as it should be in some cases, there was no evidence of a global warming hoax. But the scandal, reported widely in the media, left questions in the public's minds. By 2010, just 53 percent of Americans saw climate change as a serious threat, down 10 percent from years past, according to a Gallup poll.

President Barack Obama took office in 2009, and internationally, progress was made in December of that year. The United States and other nations signed the Copenhagen Accord, promising to lower emissions by 80 percent of 2000 levels.

This is supposed to prevent more than 3.6 degrees F (2 degrees C) of global warming. In 2015, the nations will decide if the target needs to be reduced to 2.7 degrees F (1.5 degrees C), which would require a further reduction of greenhouse gases. Developing nations like China, India, and Brazil signed the accord, an important breakthrough both environmentally, as they are now emitting a large share of the current carbon dioxide levels, and politically, as this progress was thought to be needed to get the U.S. Congress on board.

In 2009, then President-Elect Barack Obama met with Vice President–Elect Joe Biden and the former vice president Al Gore to discuss climate change, energy, and the economy. Obama has instated many policies to combat global warming.

Though the accord was not legally binding, President Obama hoped that it would be enough to persuade Congress to pass a climate bill that would have set limits on greenhouse gas emissions by businesses, through a cap and trade system. If businesses emitted less greenhouse gas than their limits, they could sell credits to companies that emitted more than their limits. The bill was supported by some power companies, including Duke Energy, General Electric, and Shell Oil. These companies wanted to invest in green energy technologies, and said that the cap and trade bill would convince investors that it was prudent to do so. The bill passed in the House but was not brought to the Senate floor, as even moderate Republicans didn't support it. Some experts blamed the economy, and others blamed politicians. But some said the American public simply didn't care enough about global warming to demand that its leaders take action. Which takes us back to the question posed in Chapter 12: Why don't people care more? Or do they? Because if you look closely, you'll find people who do care and are taking action to stop global warming. From military officers to students, these people are bypassing the debate and instead rolling up their sleeves and getting to work.

BE THE CHANGE

WHAT: *Reduce waste emissions.*

HOW: *Compost food scraps and yard waste. In a pile or enclosed bin (which some cities require), mix half dry waste (such as leaves, cardboard, and newspaper) and half wet waste (such as fruit and vegetable scraps, coffee grounds, and grass clippings). (Do not compost meat or dairy products yourself, as they'll attract rodents.) You can allow the pile to decompose* into soil on its own over several months, or turn it weekly to get soil faster. If you live in an apartment, you can compost your food scraps in a covered bin, ventilated with drilled holes. You will need the same mix of green and brown scraps, and also some soil.

WHY: Food scraps make up the largest percentage of municipal waste that is not recycled—21 percent according to the EPA. In landfills, food scraps are compacted with other trash and get little oxygen. Therefore, they emit methane when they decompose. Composting at home allows food scraps to decompose in an oxygenated environment, in which they emit less methane. Transporting food scraps to landfills also results in carbon dioxide emissions that could be avoided if you compost them at home (or through your municipal compost program, if your city has one). Finally, the resulting soil from composting can be used to grow plants that absorb more carbon dioxide.

WHAT ELSE: Use your compost to practice no-till gardening. A couple of months before planting a garden, add an 8-inch (20-centimeter) layer of leaves and other compost to your garden. This loosens the soil and also prevents weeds from growing. When it's time to plant, clear away any compost that is not decomposed into soil. Then, rather than turning over the soil in the whole garden, sow the seeds or plant the plants directly into the loosened soil. This prevents the carbon stored in the soil from being released into the air.

CHAPTER 13
A LITTLE LESS TALK,
A LOT MORE ACTION

Across the world, government leaders, businesses, and students are working to lower greenhouse gas emissions in order to ensure a healthy and happy future.

THE PRESIDENT

Though carbon cap and trade legislation failed, President Obama still worked to limit greenhouse gas emissions through the Clean Air Act. Under the Obama administration, the EPA will start by limiting the emissions at power plants. The limits will likely force coal-fired plants to capture and store the gas they emit. Carbon dioxide will be captured inside the flues (or chimneys) of power plants. There, the exhaust from coal combustion will move through a mist of chemicals. These chemicals will react with the carbon dioxide, trapping it inside the flue, while the remaining exhaust flows out into the air. The carbon dioxide will then be stored deep

Citing health concerns covered by the Clean Air Act, the EPA will limit carbon dioxide emissions at power plants.

underground. Though these carbon dioxide limits have been challenged in court, judges have ruled that global warming due to greenhouse gas emissions is a threat to public health and that gives the EPA the authority to limit emissions. The EPA will likely extend these regulations to industry. In the meantime, the EPA has worked with states to invest in wind, solar, and nuclear power, and biofuels (clean-burning fuels made from recently living things such as plant matter).

In the transportation sector, Obama is increasing fuel efficiency standards to 54.5 miles per gallon (23 kilometers per liter) by 2025 and developing fuel economy standards for diesel trucks. He also made a goal of getting one million plug-in electric vehicles (PEVs) on the road by 2016. Through the American Recovery and Reinvestment Act, he granted the

Department of Energy $400 million to build an infrastructure for electric cars, including charging stations in homes, workplaces, and public spaces. Now the major automakers are rolling out PEVs for consumers, even as they tackle the problem of the high price of batteries for electric cars. To encourage the adoption of biofuels, the U.S. Renewable Fuel Standard requires 36 billion gallons (136 billion liters) of biofuel to be produced annually by 2022.

THE MILITARY

One of the biggest proponents of combatting global warming is the U.S. military. The 2010 Defense Department Review says that climate change is already under way and that, going forward, it "will contribute to food and water scarcity, will increase the spread of disease, and may spur mass migration." To avoid the worst consequences, the military is going green by increasing efficiency and switching to clean energy.

This is a win-win decision for the military. For one thing, it will decrease the amount of fuel that needs to be transported. Moving fuel is a dangerous job; one soldier is killed for every twenty-four fuel convoys deployed. This fact inspired ex-Navy SEAL Doug Morehead to found the company Earl Energy, which makes power generators that are 93 percent more fuel efficient through their use of solar panels and highly efficient batteries. They are now being used by the Navy SEALs and in some military command centers.

The military is also going green to decrease its greenhouse gas emissions, thus helping to curb global warming. The armed forces have invested in solar, wind, and geothermal power, and in hybrid, electric, and hydrogen- and natural-gas-powered vehicles. Not only will this cut U.S. carbon emissions because of the military's size (it is our nation's largest employer), but it will also support research and development for sustainable energy products that can be adopted by civilians. For instance, the Air Force plans to use a cleaner fuel alternative for 50 percent of its aviation fuel by 2016. This transition can later be repeated by commercial aircraft companies.

The military is also preparing for climate change that is already under way. The armed forces are helping foreign militaries to prepare for natural disasters due to global warming. The U.S. military is preparing to respond to political conflicts due to land loss and food and water shortages. The military is also securing its own bases from the effects of climate change, as thirty installations are currently threatened by rising sea level.

CITY GOVERNMENTS

In 2005, 141 mayors signed the Climate Protection Agreement, the goal of which is for each of their cities to meet the Kyoto Protocol goal of reducing greenhouse gas emissions by 7 percent of 1990 levels. By 2013, more than one thousand mayors had signed on.

Because of compact living and use of public transportation, the carbon footprint of the average New Yorker is 71 percent smaller than that of the average U.S. citizen. City leadership has made the city even greener.

One mayor who went above and beyond to green his city was Mike Bloomberg, in New York City. The city was already one of the greenest in America due to its compactness. People who live and work in small areas require less gasoline for their commutes, and in fact, many New Yorkers do not own cars but walk or take public transportation. (Even taking a taxi in New York has little environmental impact, as the majority of new taxis are hybrids.) Those living in small apartments consume less electricity and fewer goods (which require energy to make). And choosing to live in the city, as opposed to a new suburb, decreases the demand for new developments to be built on wild lands. As a result, the carbon footprint of the average New Yorker is one-third that of the average U.S. citizen.[29]

On top of that, under the leadership of Bloomberg, the

city planted more than eight hundred thousand trees, with a goal of planting one million total. Trees store carbon dioxide and also provide shade, reducing summer temperatures in the city and thus the need for air conditioning. Bloomberg also launched the collection of food waste for compost. At the same time, the city continues to upgrade its infrastructure to account for a rise in sea level.

Many other cities are also combatting global warming. In San Francisco, half the taxis are alternative-fuel vehicles, 70 percent of waste is composted or recycled, and half of all residents commute to work by biking, walking, or taking public transportation. Portland has changed its zoning regulations to encourage compact developments that require little driving. Seattle gets 90 percent of its electricity from its rivers in the form of hydropower and is educating its residents about energy efficiency at home. Chicago has installed more than ten thousand bike racks, created 114 miles of bike lanes, and grown more square feet of rooftop gardens than all other cities combined. The list of green measures being taken in cities across America goes on and on.

STATE GOVERNMENTS

States are also taking action on climate change, sometimes enacting laws ahead of the federal government. Case in point: While Congress failed to pass a cap and trade bill in 2010, California passed its own legislation in 2012. And New England's program has been in place for more than a decade. Likewise, in 2007, Congress failed to pass a national standard that would have required utilities to use a certain percentage of clean energy. Yet more than half of U.S. states already mandate this, California leading the way with a one-third clean energy requirement. Even when conservative groups (funded by the fossil fuel industry) have lobbied to repeal these laws, states with a Republican majority have kept them in place. The reasons are easy to see. The laws have created jobs. For instance, Texas established a renewable portfolio standard under Governor George W. Bush in 1999 (before he became president). This created jobs in the wind turbine industry and provided additional income to farmers who installed turbines on their land. The state is now the largest wind producer in the United States. In addition, there are now more Texans working in the solar energy sector than there are ranchers.

States are also leading the way in reducing vehicle emissions. California has enacted several laws to this end, including the Zero Emission Vehicle Regulation, which requires automakers to produce a certain number of zero-emission vehicles each year. In 2010, California passed a low-carbon fuel standard, which requires fuel providers to reduce the carbon intensity of transportation fuels by 10 percent by 2020 (carbon intensity is the amount of carbon emitted per unit of energy used). Providers can meet the standard by adding low-carbon fuel to their fuel mix. For instance, they could add certain biofuels to their gasoline or diesel fuel. Fuel providers can also purchase credits from clean energy providers, such as electric companies that power vehicles with clean energy. In this way, the program will help clean energy companies to grow. Washington and Oregon are now considering low-carbon fuel standards as well.

BUSINESSES

For business leaders, reducing greenhouse gas emissions combines stewardship with good business sense. Tony Malkin, owner of the Empire State Building, sought to reduce energy use in the building through a retrofit project. In the process, he hoped to demonstrate how others could do the same — and save money. The retrofit included new energy-efficient windows, changes to the heating and cooling systems, and a program that allows tenants to monitor their energy use on the Web. These renovations decreased energy use by 38 percent — a savings of $4.4 million per year. Other building owners are taking note; tours of the Empire State Building have spawned interest in similar retrofits, and projects are under way around the world.

James Peret wanted to help smaller businesses save money on energy. Working out of his garage, he developed the Vegawatt, an electricity generator that runs on recycled vegetable oil. Restaurants that specialize in fried foods can generate 80 gallons (303 liters) of used oil each week. That can be converted to five kilowatts of energy an hour, for a savings of $1,000 per month. The units pay for themselves within a couple of years—or sooner where alternative energy grants are available.

Likewise, some farmers are converting manure to electricity. Shawn Saylor, a dairy farmer in Pennsylvania, installed such a system through a grant from the Pennsylvania Department of Energy and was able to convert 18,000 gallons (68,137 liters) of manure produced daily by his six hundred cows into energy to power his entire farm, saving $60,000 annually. He even had leftover power to sell to the power company. In addition to reducing fossil-fuel-powered electricity use, recycling manure reduces the methane and nitrous oxide that it would otherwise release into the atmosphere.

STUDENTS

Each year, the president recognizes young people making a difference in the Environmental Youth Awards. Several 2012 winners focused on reducing greenhouse gas emissions. Students at Camden Hills Regional High School in Maine improved their school's energy efficiency, and then raised funds to construct a wind turbine that supplies 10–20 percent of the school's electricity. Likewise, students at Mahtomedi High School in Minnesota helped to raise $100,000 to build a wind turbine that powers their athletic stadium and educates the community about wind energy.

The Net Zero Club at Fairview High School in Colorado

Kids who won environmental awards.

lobbied the Boulder City Council to place a ten-cent fee on plastic and paper bags. Though a nominal amount, such fees have been credited with changing people's habits when it comes to using plastic bags. In Ireland, a tax the equivalent of 33 U.S. cents per bag lowered plastic bag use by 94 percent, largely because it made such bags socially unacceptable. In Boulder, the fee is forecasted to reduce the number of bags used per year by ten million. This will reduce not only litter but also the emissions caused by manufacturing and transporting the plastic bags.

THE WORLD

The Copenhagen Accord, negotiated on December 18, 2009, was an important first step toward addressing global warming as a united world. The United States and 140 other nations pledged to lower world emissions in order to avoid more than a 3.6-degree-F (2-degree-C) rise in global temperature. Commitments vary from nation to nation and are based on legislation that is already under way in each country. For instance, America has pledged to reduce its emissions to 17 percent below 2005 levels by 2020, 42 percent by 2030, and 83 percent by 2050. To achieve the first goal, America is working toward limiting carbon dioxide emissions at power plants, increasing fuel efficiency, and reducing methane emissions in the natural gas industry. The World Resources Institute says that these and other state and executive actions could allow America to meet its 2020 and 2030 Copenhagen targets. But for the United States to meet its 2050 goal, new laws will be needed, and that will require Congress to act.

Other countries are taking similar legislative measures to meet their 2020 goals. For instance, China has pledged to reduce its emissions to 40 to 45 percent below 2005 levels per unit of Gross Domestic Product (GDP). GDP is the total value of goods and services that a nation produces and provides. So in China, the more goods and services the nation produces, the more greenhouse gases it can emit. This allows the economy to continue to grow. To meet this goal, China pledges to shift to 15 percent non-fossil-fuel energy and to add 99 million acres (40 million hectares) of forest by 2020, among other actions.

India pledged to reduce emissions by 20 to 25 percent of

2005 levels per unit of GDP by developing building efficiency codes, adding forest lands, and increasing renewable energy to 20 percent by 2020. Brazil pledged to bring its emissions down to 1994 levels by 2020, in part by reducing deforestation by 80 percent of peak levels. The European Union, a leader in addressing climate change, has already met its Kyoto Protocol pledge of reducing greenhouse gas emissions by 8 percent of 1990 levels. Its Copenhagen commitment is to reduce emissions by 20 percent of 1990 levels by 2020, and possibly to increase that pledge to 30 percent. In addition, developed countries pledged financial aid to developing nations so that they could curb deforestation and prepare for the effects of climate change.

Smaller nations are also doing their part to address climate change. Costa Rican leaders declared that the nation would be carbon neutral by 2021, meaning that any carbon dioxide released would be absorbed in the same amount (by forests, for instance). To achieve that, Costa Rica tackled its agriculture emissions, which make up 37 percent of its emissions. Small farmers are now taught to use recycled agricultural waste as fertilizer in lieu of synthetic fertilizer, which releases nitrous oxide. Large banana farms protect acres of rainforest in order to offset the greenhouse gases emitted while transporting bananas. Cattle and pig ranchers capture methane from manure and use this gas as fuel. The country also gets 90 percent of its electricity from sustainable sources, mainly hydroelectric, but also wind power and geothermal. Granted, Costa Rica produces only a small portion of the world's greenhouse gas emissions, but it is setting an impressive example for other nations.

In addition, the United States and China are working toward amending the Montreal Protocol (the treaty that saved the ozone layer by banning chlorofluorocarbons). New rules would ban some hydrofluorocarbons as well. These chemicals, which took the place of chlorofluorocarbons, can be extremely potent greenhouse gases. The World Research Institute says that negotiating their phase-out is one of the most important things the United States can do to combat global warming.

Experts say the Copenhagen commitments are a good start but not sufficient to meet the goal of preventing more than a 3.6-degree-F (2-degree-C) rise. They hope that nations will step up their commitments each time they meet. To keep carbon dioxide levels below 450 parts per million in hopes of meeting this climate goal, the world will need to address deforestation and agricultural emissions. But the most important change, particularly in America, will be to transform energy. In short, we need to become more energy efficient and switch to greener energy sources.

There is still much to be done. You need only look at the rising carbon dioxide levels measured at Mauna Loa (391.83 parts per million in December 2011, 394.28 parts per million in December 2012, 396.81 parts per million in December 2013) to see that more action is needed. The good news is that we have everything we need to reduce greenhouse gas emissions right here, right now.

BE THE CHANGE

WHAT: *Reduce waste emissions.*

HOW: *Eat leftovers. Take leftovers in your lunch or repurpose them as soup the next night.*

WHY: *American families throw away 25 percent of their food and drinks, at a loss of up to $2,275 per year for a family of four.[30] This food waste makes up 14.5 percent of municipal waste and contributes to methane emissions at landfills. Meat and dairy scraps cannot be composted at home, but they can be eaten! Not only does this reduce methane emissions at landfills, it also reduces the greenhouse gases emitted in the process of growing food. And it saves money.*

WHAT ELSE: *Start with small servings. If you're still hungry, take more. That way, food from the pot can be saved as leftovers (whereas your family may be reluctant to save leftovers from the plate due to germs).*

PART FIVE
LET'S DO THIS!

CHAPTER 14
BE EFFICIENT.
B. E. EFFICIENT

ENERGY POWERS OUR HOMES, WORKPLACES, and vehicles. To live healthy lives in a modern society, we need energy. But how *much* we need depends on efficiency. As it is, we use a lot of energy. The average American uses approximately ten kilowatts of electricity each day. In *Earth: The Operators' Manual*, the author Richard Alley shows what that means in terms of human energy. One hundred watts equal 2,000 calories of human energy, the amount most people burn in a day. This means that the average American uses 240,000 calories per day. It would be impossible to exert that much energy in one day, so without electricity, modern life would in fact require each of us to have more than one hundred servants. Thankfully, there are many ways to reduce our energy consumption.

energy use.[31] Half of this energy is used in homes. Home energy use has climbed through the years because, for one thing, houses are getting bigger. Since 1950, living space per person has more than doubled, requiring more heating and cooling, two of the biggest energy factors in homes.

Air conditioning, a rarity in the 1950s, now exists in 84 percent of all U.S. homes. Powered by electricity (the majority of which is derived from fossil fuels in the United States), air conditioning adds 110 million tons (100 million metric tons) of carbon dioxide to the atmosphere each year. The majority of homes in America are heated with natural gas, a fossil fuel (albeit a cleaner-burning fuel than coal or oil). Electricity

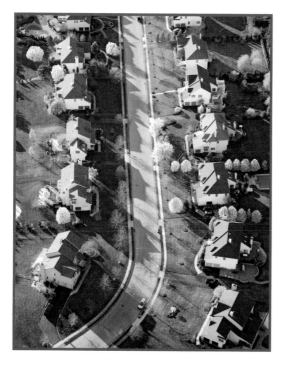

Homes built today are bigger than in the past. Since 1950, the living space per person in the United States has more than doubled.

is the second largest provider of heat. Propane and heating oil are third and fourth on the list, and these are also fossil fuels. Needless to say, greater heating and cooling use results in greater greenhouse gas emissions. Homes also have more appliances, including computers, cell phones, multiple TVs, and microwaves. More efficient appliances under the Energy Star program have reduced the impact, but haven't made up for the growing number of appliances and added floor space.

To increase home efficiency, experts suggest starting with the "low-hanging fruit"—the easy things that cost nothing and actually save money. They include replacing incandescent light bulbs with fluorescent or LED bulbs, unplugging appliances when not in use, and turning the thermostat up in the summer and down in the winter. But curbing energy use is sort of like eating healthy. Most people know that they should do it. The challenge is making it a habit. Some states are asking utility companies to help homeowners change their energy habits.

Pacific Gas & Electric in California, for instance, is allowing homeowners to track their energy use online so that they can see and eliminate wasteful habits. Customers can also compare their energy use from day to day and week to week. So if they change a habit, such as shutting down computers at night, they can see the effects on their energy use right away. The utility also charges more for electricity during peak hours, which encourages energy use during off-peak hours. Pacific Gas & Electric is working toward a smart grid, which is a computerized electricity system. Both electrical companies and consumers will be able to track energy use and make changes to conserve energy. This grid will rely more heavily on renewable energy. When peak energy use is lowered, renewable energy sources can better meet demands. Plug-in electric vehicles would fit nicely into the grid, allowing homeowners to charge their vehicles during off-peak times, and to use the energy stored in the battery to power their homes if they do not plan on driving that day.

Next, experts recommend that the government set higher efficiency standards for appliances, windows, and insulation. The effects of higher standards are great. Since California instituted high efficiency standards in the 1970s, their energy use has stayed flat per capita even as the economy grew. Experts also recommend that homes be built or retrofitted to be more efficient. Passivhaus (passive house) home designs, created by the engineer Dr. Wolfgang Feist, are a good example of what is possible. These homes, more than twenty-five thousand of which have been built in Europe, are net zero. They are so well insulated and the windows so energy efficient that they do not require furnaces. This makes the homes affordable even with so many energy upgrades.

SMARTER BUILDINGS

The same habits can be applied in schools and workplaces, where energy and money savings can really add up. If all workers powered down their computers at the end of the day, for instance, they would reduce carbon dioxide emissions by 22 million tons (20 million metric tons) and save a collective $2.8 billion.[32] A school that turned off computers at night and the lights in unoccupied rooms could save thousands of dollars each year. The Seattle School District saved $20,000 in a year just by turning off vending machine lights at night.

To save more energy, experts recommend making changes to older buildings. We saw the dramatic effects that a $106

Greece's iconic white walls reflect sunlight, making buildings cooler. White roofs in U.S. cities would reduce the need for air conditioning, making buildings more efficient.

million energy upgrade had on the Empire State Building. Smaller changes can also save energy and money. Painting a rooftop white can cool a building, reducing the energy spent on air conditioning. Done on a larger scale, it could reduce the temperature of an entire city. If Los Angeles required light-colored roofs and paving, and planted more trees, it could reduce the heat in the city by 5 degrees F (2.9 degrees C).[33] (This known cooling effect is one reason for Greece's iconic whitewashed buildings.)

For new construction, companies are finding that energy-efficient buildings are no more expensive to build and can save money. For this reason, many schools are now going green. After an F5 tornado 1.7 miles (2.7 kilometers) wide leveled Greensburg, Kansas, in 2007, civic leaders decided to rebuild the entire town with a focus on sustainability. The K–12 grade school was built to let in natural sunlight and heat, to recycle rainwater, and to use 100 percent renewable energy (mainly wind power). Because of its efficiency, the school didn't need to install a boiler or heating equipment, which offset the price of energy upgrades. Now the school saves about $150,000 per year on energy.

TRANSFORM TRANSPORTATION

Vehicles will also need to be more efficient in order to fit into a world run on clean energy. President Obama raised U.S. efficiency standards to 54.5 miles per gallon (23.2 km/L) by 2025. The World Research Institute says that to meet its Copenhagen goals, the United States needs to continue to increase efficiency so that cars get 92 miles per gallon (39.1 km/L) by 2035. In addition, state policies could encourage more efficient transportation systems. For instance, neighborhoods can be designed so that schools, homes, workplaces, shopping areas, and sporting fields are closer together, requiring less driving. Public transportation, bike paths, and highway carpool lanes can also be created at the state and local level.

However, fuel efficiency alone won't be enough. Vehicles will also need to run on clean-burning fuel or clean electricity. Daniel Sperling, director of the Institute of Transportation Studies at the University of California, Davis, says that the shift will be gradual but that policies are in place for the United States to switch almost entirely to alternative-fuel vehicles by 2050. The leading candidates for alternative-fuel vehicles are PEVs, biofuel vehicles, and fuel cell vehicles.

PEVs rely on a battery that is charged by plugging the car into an electrical outlet. PEVs are already on the market, but manufacturers are trying to develop a more affordable battery in order to bring down the price. Fuel cell vehicles also have electric motors, but rather than being plugged in, the cars generate their own electricity. The vehicles are filled up at the pump with hydrogen fuel. The hydrogen combines with oxygen in the air, and this chemical reaction powers the battery. Fuel cell vehicles emit no carbon dioxide. To make fuel cell

Plug-in electric vehicles powered by renewable electricity are one alternative to gasoline-powered cars. The other leading alternatives are fuel cell vehicles and biofuel vehicles. All are promising but have obstacles to overcome.

technology truly carbon-free, the hydrogen fuel needs to be produced through green energy. Fuel cell vehicles exist today but, like PEVs, are expensive to build. Fuel cell technology is considered the least far along of the three options discussed here.

Biofuel vehicles are similar to gasoline- and diesel-powered vehicles in that both have internal combustion engines and are filled up at the pump. Biofuels are already being blended with fossil fuels. Most vehicles today can run on up to 10 percent ethanol (a biofuel) mixed with gasoline, or 5 percent

Vehicles could easily be engineered to run on biofuel. The challenge is in finding biofuel that is itself eco-friendly. Elephant grass, shown here, is one such option.

biodiesel mixed with diesel fuel. In Brazil, vehicles must be built to run on at least 25 percent biofuel, and 17 percent of all vehicles are flex-fuel vehicles, meaning they can run on up to 85 percent biofuel. In America, only a little more than 3 percent of vehicles are flex-fuel vehicles, but that is expected to grow. Manufacturing flex-fuel vehicles is estimated to cost only $50–$100 more per vehicle than standard-fuel vehicles.[34] Transitioning to biofuel vehicles sounds easy enough. But the challenge is in producing biofuel without emitting too much carbon dioxide. We'll look at that challenge in the next chapter.

Each alternative-fuel vehicle has challenges to overcome,

but also exciting potential. The world will likely switch to all three, with their prevalence varying from nation to nation, according to Sperling.

REUSE, REDUCE, RECYCLE. REALLY.

Another way to increase efficiency is to recycle, which cuts down on the energy required to make new products. You likely recycle at home and school, and that's important. But it might give you the idea that the United States recycles a large percentage of its waste. Unfortunately, that's not the case. The average American produces 4.4 total pounds (2 kilograms) of municipal waste (through our homes, schools, hospitals, and businesses) per day and recycles or composts 1.53 pounds (0.69 kilograms) of that. So we are recycling 34.7 percent of our waste. In contrast, Austria recycles or composts 63 percent of its municipal waste, and Germany, 62 percent.

European Union countries have achieved such high rates, in part, by composting. Austria composts 34 percent of its municipal waste, and Germany, 17 percent. Composting municipal waste reduces greenhouse gases in two ways. First, it reduces methane emissions at landfills. Second, it reduces carbon dioxide emissions by garbage trucks. Compost sites tend to be much closer to the city of collection than landfills, which are often in other states. In America, food waste and yard trimmings combined make up 28 percent of municipal waste. All of that could be composted. Indeed, that's what cities like San Francisco, Seattle, Portland, and New York are already doing. In San Francisco, only 22 percent of municipal waste winds up in landfills — the rest is recycled or composted. The city's goal is to send zero waste to landfills by 2020.

Now, what if *everything* could be recycled? Stained clothing. Musty carpeting. Worn-out shoes. Broken computers. The thing is, it can be. And this process cuts down on greenhouse gases emitted by industry. Because instead of starting from scratch — with plants or minerals — industry can manufacture goods with recycled textile, rubber, or metal, and that requires less energy. Clothing recycling, in particular, is on the rise, with some cities offering curbside pickup for items too torn and tattered to be donated. Queen Creek, Arizona, for instance, sells textiles collected curbside to a company that recycles them for use as insulation. If these programs became more widespread, 11.1 million tons (10 million metric tons) of textiles could be diverted from landfills, and emissions could be reduced in the textile industry.

Businesses have found that it makes environmental and financial sense to recycle. The steel industry recycles 88 percent of the steel it manufactures. Because steel is a key material used to build cars, the automobile industry has a 92.5 percent recycling rate. Computer companies are also starting to recycle more of their products. Dell, IBM, and Hewlett-Packard collect computers and copiers for recycling, and Staples accepts computers of any brand for recycling. But so much more

With recycled materials, we can create things like this play structure and enrich communities in two different ways.

could be done. With a shift in thinking, *everything*—from packaging to electronics to industrial chemicals—could be reused, recycled, or composted.

BE THE CHANGE

WHAT: Reduce household emissions.

HOW: Unplug appliances when they are not in use rather than merely turning them off.

WHY: When plugged in but off, appliances and computers can still account for 10 percent of home electricity use. If you unplug these items when not in use, you'll not only conserve energy today, but those of you who become engineers may develop smarter appliances that by design conserve energy when not in use.

WHAT ELSE: Power down computers, tablets, and cell phones. It takes a little more energy to start a computer than it does to keep it running, but if you will not be using it for two hours, you will save energy by turning it off. At night, the power strip for all computers and printers should be turned off.

BE THE CHANGE

WHAT: Reduce industry emissions.

HOW: Before you throw something away, find out if it can be recycled. You'd be surprised what can be. Clothing, carpeting, shoes, and even surfboards are collected at certain drop-off points.

WHY: Recycling reduces industry emissions because manufacturers don't need to start from scratch with raw ingredients, but rather have usable material to make goods.

WHAT ELSE: Offer to take friends' or families' items to the recycling drop-off point, or organize a recycling drive for the items at school. This not only results in more items being recycled, but also raises awareness about what can be recycled.

CHAPTER 15
WITH GREAT POWER COMES
GREAT RESPONSIBILITY

If we improve efficiency, we can realistically power the world with clean energy. Clean energy is abundant. Sunshine from the Arizona desert could power the United States, and sunshine from the Sahara could power the rest of the world.[35] Building the infrastructure to capture this energy and convert it into electricity is under way, but it will take time and money to complete. Likewise, alternative fuels are already on the market, but a wholesale shift to alternative-fuel cars, trucks, trains, ships, and airplanes will be gradual. Here is a rundown of what is available in terms of green energy.

EARTH

Geothermal energy is the heat stored underground. It can be used for heat or electricity (in which case, steam from deep underground propels a turbine that produces electric power). Geothermal power supplies less than 1 percent of electricity

The Mammoth Pacific power plant in Casa Diablo, California, is one of many geothermal plants in the state.

in the United States, but experts believe there is potential for more in the western states. Already, the Geysers, steam fields in Northern California, produce 60 percent of the electricity typically used along the coast from the Golden Gate Bridge to the Oregon border. The United States is currently the largest producer of geothermal power.

WIND

Wind power is produced by turbines, which can be installed on land or over water. A growing source of electricity in America, wind powers eleven million homes, with turbines

Wind turbines are becoming a more common sight in the United States. Wind powers 11 million homes in America, and a few thousand turbines are added to the grid each year.

being added to the grid each year (3,464 just in 2011). According to the Natural Resources Defense Council, wind could supply 30 percent of America's electricity. Currently, it provides 6 percent during peak months, with leading wind energy states being Texas, California, and Iowa. To power the world with wind power, ten million turbines would be needed. This would require the construction of a thousand per day over thirty years. It's more likely that wind power will be combined with solar and other forms of renewable energy to meet the world's energy needs.

SUN

Solar energy can be derived from space or from solar panels on Earth. Space-based solar panels would absorb the sun's energy and transmit it to Earth via microwaves (electromagnetic waves, not the ovens you cook burritos in). Space-based solar technology is available, but is not yet in use. Earthbound solar panels, on the other hand, are already quite common.

Some solar panels are installed on homes or buildings to provide power to that one location. In Hawaii, where electricity prices are high, 10 percent of homes have these types of solar panels. Solar panels may become as accessible as window-unit air conditioners. Some companies are

Solar panels can be installed on rooftops or at solar power plants. In the future, they may also be stationed in space.

developing solar panels that you can buy at a home improvement store and install yourself. To connect one to your power grid, you simply plug the system into your power outlet. To accept power from home-based sources, grids will require upgrades. In Hawaii, solar panels were installed so rapidly that they began to overwhelm the power grid, creating a danger to utility workers. Upgrades to the power grid were needed before more could be installed.

Solar panels can also be centralized at power plants. In India, for instance, a 4-gigawatt solar plant is being constructed over 23,000 acres (9,308 hectares). If a similar plant were built in America, it would provide power to three million homes. According to a study by University of California, Berkeley, solar energy could affordably supply one-third of the power in all states west of Kansas by 2050. The same study showed that other renewables, like wind and geothermal power, could meet most of the remaining needs, allowing the United States to reduce emissions by 80 percent compared to 1990 levels.

WATER

Hydroelectric power comes from the energy of flowing water gathered through turbines at large dams. The largest source of renewable energy, it supplies 7 percent of the electricity in America. Worldwide, it provides 19 percent of all electricity. Most good hydropower sites in America are already in use, but worldwide, two-thirds of the available hydropower has

Hydropower supplies 19 percent of electricity worldwide. One example of hydropower is the Hoover Dam, which sits on the border of Arizona and Nevada and harnesses the power of the Colorado River to supply energy to parts of Arizona, Nevada, and California.

yet to be developed.[36] The drawback to hydropower is that it requires the construction of dams, which are disruptive to wildlife in rivers and people living beside rivers.

Other water-based sources of energy include tidal and current power, for which turbines are placed underwater to harness the energy of tides and currents. The world's first commercial tidal turbine was installed in 2008 at Strangford Lough in Northern Ireland. It consists of two large turbines that generate 1.2 megawatts of energy, enough to power 1,500 homes.

NUCLEAR POWER

Nuclear power comes from splitting the uranium atom in a process known as nuclear fission. (Uranium is a naturally occurring heavy metal.) The heat derived from splitting the atom drives turbines that create electricity. Eventually, nuclear fusion may also be used to produce power. In that case, the nuclei of two atoms are joined, producing one large nucleus and a great deal of energy. The United States is the largest producer of nuclear power; it supplies 19 percent of our electricity.[37] France is the second biggest producer. There, it supplies a whopping 75 percent of the country's electricity.

Nuclear energy gets a bad rap because of accidents such as the Fukushima Daiichi disaster, in which a 2011 tsunami in Japan caused a nuclear power plant meltdown. However, scientists believe nuclear energy provides a safer alternative to coal. Coal-fired plants cause 100,000 deaths per year worldwide due to air pollution[38], whereas scientists estimate that the Fukushima meltdown will cause a total of 15 to 1,300 premature deaths in the long run[39]. That said, funding is difficult because nuclear power plants are expensive and time consuming to build, and if a meltdown or near-meltdown occurs anywhere in the world, the project may be canceled due to public outcry. But as seen in France, nuclear energy is plentiful, and with government policies that encourage loans, it could make up a sizable portion of our energy in the future.

WASTE

There are many ways to recycle waste for energy. One way is to capture greenhouse gases at landfills. In the United States,

570 out of 2,400 municipal solid waste landfills capture and recycle methane gases for energy. The EPA is trying to increase that number through its Landfill Methane Outreach Program. When the methane is converted to energy, it breaks down into water and carbon dioxide. So carbon dioxide is still released, but that is a much less potent gas than methane.

Another form of waste recycling is plasma arc technology. Developed at Georgia Institute of Technology, it is being implemented in Japan and in some U.S. states. Waste in landfills is heated to high temperatures, converting organic materials to fuel. Inorganic materials, such as metals, become rocks that can be used in construction. Fuel produced in this way burns much cleaner than coal and oil; it releases about the same amount of greenhouse emissions as natural gas.

BIOFUELS

Biofuels are fuels made with recently living things. This includes corn, agricultural waste, wood chips, bacteria, algae, animal fats, and more. Biofuels emit little carbon dioxide when burned. However, the carbon dioxide emitted during their production has to be considered. For instance, if a forest were cleared to grow plants to produce biofuel, then that would result in carbon dioxide emissions. Also, using food crops such as corn for biofuel is considered unethical because the increased demand for these crops drives up food prices worldwide. Biofuels with low carbon footprints include plant waste and plants that store carbon while being grown. Switchgrass, for instance, is an American prairie grass that stores carbon dioxide in its long roots. Another upside of switchgrass is that it can be grown on land unsuitable for agriculture. In that way, it doesn't compete with food crops for land. Technologies are being developed to convert this type of biomass into fuel.

ALL HANDS ON DECK

A combination of these renewable resources will be needed if we are to replace or mostly replace fossil fuels. Likewise, a combined effort by world leaders, local governments, businesses, and people like us will be needed to tackle climate change. It will be the challenge of the century. But it will also be the opportunity of a lifetime as new jobs and entrepreneurial opportunities open up in the field of renewable energy.

What will your role be? Will you invent a more efficient system of capturing and storing carbon dioxide? Will you push through legislation that leads to the shift toward all electric or biofuel cars? Will you bring wind energy to your state, or composting to your town? Perhaps you will show your company how to save boatloads of money by being more efficient. Or become the Rockefeller of biofuels. Or a Batman-like solar energy magnate. Maybe you will teach people how to grow food in a way that emits fewer greenhouse gases. Or teach a kid how to plant a tree. Whatever you decide to do, always remember that you are the change the world needs. It's up to you. It's up to all of us.

BE THE CHANGE

WHAT: Spread the word.

HOW: Talk about what you're doing. Share the practical ways you are "being the change." Offer tips for composting, saving energy at home, and walking or biking to school.

WHY: Sometimes all people need to change is a little practical advice.

WHAT ELSE: Become politically active. Attend school, town, or state meetings where matters related to global warming are being discussed. Let your elected officials know you care about the public health matter that is global warming.

GLOSSARY

Agricultural Revolution. The shift that humans made from hunting and gathering to growing plants and raising animals.

anthropogenic. Caused by humans, as in "dangerous anthropogenic interference."

Big Bang. An event that led the universe to expand from a hot, dense state, according to the prevailing scientific theory.

biofuel. Fuel derived from recently living things.

black carbon. Soot; particulate matter that traps heat in the atmosphere similarly to how greenhouse gases trap heat.

carbon cap and trade. Types of programs that limit the amount of greenhouse gases that companies can emit, and that allow companies that emit less than their limits to sell credits to companies that emit more than their limits.

carbon dioxide. A greenhouse gas that occurs naturally in the atmosphere and that also is emitted through human activities.

carbon-14. The radioactive carbon that occurs naturally in the environment and has also been released through nuclear bomb testing. It differs from fossil carbon, which is no longer radioactive.

carbon intensity. The amount of carbon emitted per unit of energy used (of a fuel).

climate. The weather in a given place observed over time.

Copenhagen Accord. An agreement between many of the world's nations to reduce greenhouse gas emissions by specific amounts.

fluorinated gases. Several different greenhouse gases, which make up only a small percentage of greenhouse gas emissions but are much better at trapping heat than carbon dioxide.

fossil fuels. Fuels formed over many years by the remains of living things. They include coal, oil, and natural gas.

fuel cell vehicle. A vehicle that is fueled by a battery that is powered by the chemical reaction of hydrogen and oxygen.

geothermal power. Energy derived from the heat stored underground.

glacial period. During an ice age, one of the cold phases during which glaciers expand.

glacier. A slowly moving mass of ice that forms over time due to accumulated snowfall.

global warming. The gradual increase in the earth's average temperature, caused mainly by greenhouse gas emissions.

greenhouse effect. The way that certain gases in the earth's atmosphere trap heat.

greenhouse gas emissions. Heat-trapping gases that are released into the earth's atmosphere through activities such as burning fossil fuels and clearing forests.

hydroelectric power. Energy derived from water flowing through turbines built in dams.

ice age. A period of extensive glaciers in the North and South Pole areas.

ice sheet. Glacial ice that covers more than 20,000 square miles (50,000 square kilometers). Only two ice sheets currently exist—in Antarctica and on Greenland.

Industrial Revolution. The rapid change in the economy due to the introduction of powered machinery.

interglacial period. During an ice age, one of the warmer phases during which glaciers recede.

IPCC. The Intergovernmental Panel on Climate Change; a body of scientists created by the United Nations to study climate change.

Kyoto Protocol. An international agreement to reduce greenhouse gas emissions.

low-carbon fuel standard. A law requiring fuel providers to reduce the carbon intensity of transportation fuels.

Mauna Loa Observatory. A National Oceanic and Atmospheric Administration station in Hawaii that measures carbon dioxide in the atmosphere.

methane. A greenhouse gas twenty-one times more powerful than carbon dioxide.

methane ice. Methane hydrate; methane clathrate; a chemical compound that forms when methane combines with water in cold, high-pressure environments.

Milankovitch cycles. The changes in the earth's orbit (eccentricity), tilt (obliquity), and wobble (precession), which can cause the climate to change over time.

nitrous oxide. A greenhouse gas much less prevalent but three hundred times more potent than carbon dioxide.

ocean acidification. The increase in carbonic acid in ocean water caused by increased amounts of carbon dioxide.

ozone. The layer in the atmosphere that protects the earth from UV rays.

paleoclimatologist. A scientist who studies the climates of the distant past.

parts per million. One molecule per million total molecules.

permafrost. The layer of soil in cold regions that remains frozen year-round.

Permian-Triassic extinction. An extinction event that occurred 251 million years ago.

PETM. Paleocene-Eocene Thermal Maximum; an extinction event that occurred fifty-eight to fifty-six million years ago.

plug-in electric vehicles (PEVs). Vehicles that rely on batteries that are charged by plugging the vehicles into electrical outlets.

positive feedback. Factors that cause a cooling climate to become colder or a warming climate to become warmer.

renewable energy. An energy source that is replenished quickly. It includes sunlight, wind, and water.

renewable portfolio standard. A law that requires electrical utilities to buy a certain percentage of renewable energy.

smart grid. An electricity system that thrives on efficiency, uses renewable energy sources, and allows homeowners to monitor their energy use online.

solar power. Energy derived from the sun.

water vapor. The gaseous form of water; a greenhouse gas that occurs naturally and is not directly caused by human activities.

weather. The atmospheric state in a given place and time.

wind turbine. A wheel atop a pole that rotates in the wind, generating power.

FOR FURTHER READING

BOOKS:

Gore, Al. *An Inconvenient Truth: The Crisis of Global Warming*. New York: Viking, 2007.

Flannery, Tim. Adapted by Sally M. Walker. *We Are the Weather Makers: The History of Climate Change*. New York: Candlewick, 2010.

WEBSITES:

co2now.org

Stay on top of how much carbon dioxide is being released into the atmosphere, and learn more about global warming.

cmi.princeton.edu/wedges

See what leaders can do to slow or stop global warming.

www.pbs.org/programs/earth-the-operators-manual

Learn about people who are making a difference in the fight against global warming.

us.fsc.org

Learn about the Forest Stewardship Council and its certified label.

rameznaam.com/2013/04/28/the-evidence-on-gmo-safety

Learn more about the scientific viewpoint on the safety of GMOs.

NOTES

1. Wilkinson et al., *Current Biology.*
2. Energy Star, "What About Clothes Dryers?"
3. Corell, "Global Climate Change and Water Resources Keynote."
4. Intergovernmental Panel on Climate Change, "Summary for Policymakers," 2013.
5. Ibid.
6. Ibid.
7. Lord, *Early Warming.*
8. Barclay, *National Geographic News.*
9. Weber et al., *Environmental Science & Technology.*
10. Etheridge et al., *Journal of Geophysical Research.*
11. Bond et al., *Journal of Geophysical Research.*
12. World Bank, "CO_2 Emissions (Metric Tons per Capita)."
13. Galuszka, *New York Times.*
14. Chen et al., *Lancet.*
15. Gordon et al., *Lancet Respiratory Medicine.*
16. LeBeau, *CNBC.*
17. Federal Aviation Administration, "FAA Forecast Predicts Air Travel to Double in Two Decades."
18. *BBC News,* "Brazil Says Amazon Deforestation Rose 28% in a Year."
19. Diamond, *New York Times.*
20. Intergovernmental Panel on Climate Change, "Summary for Policymakers," 2013.
21. Poore et al., U.S. Geological Survey.
22. Intergovernmental Panel on Climate Change, "Summary for Policymakers," 2007.
23. Seager et al., *Science.*
24. Intergovernmental Panel on Climate Change, "Summary for Policymakers," 2007.
25. Kolbert, *Field Notes from a Catastrophe.*

26. Mayer, "Big Oil, Big Influence."

27. Kolbert, *Field Notes from a Catastrophe.*

28. Mayer, "Big Oil, Big Influence."

29. City of New York, *Inventory of New York City Greenhouse Gas Emissions, September 2011.*

30. Gunders, Natural Resources Defense Council.

31. Lovins, *Reinventing Fire.*

32. Alliance to Save Energy, "PC Energy Report."

33. Lovins, *Reinventing Fire.*

34. Ogden and Anderson, *Sustainable Transportation Energy Pathways.*

35. Alley, *Earth: The Operators' Manual.*

36. U.S. Geological Survey, "Hydroelectric Power Water Use."

37. World Nuclear Association, "Nuclear Power in the USA."

38. Windridge, *Guardian.*

39. Black, *BBC News.*

SELECT BIBLIOGRAPHY

BOOKS

Alley, Richard B. *Earth: The Operators' Manual.* New York: Norton, 2011.

Friedman, Thomas. *Hot, Flat, and Crowded.* New York: Farrar, Straus and Giroux, 2008.

Gingrich, Newt, and Terry L. Maple. *A Contract with the Earth.* Baltimore: Johns Hopkins University Press, 2007.

Guzman, Andrew. *Overheated: The Human Cost of Climate Change.* Oxford: Oxford University Press, 2013.

Hengeveld, Rob. *Wasted World.* Chicago: University of Chicago Press, 2012.

Kolbert, Elizabeth. *Field Notes from a Catastrophe.* New York: Bloomsbury, 2006.

Lord, Nancy. *Early Warning.* Berkeley, CA: Counterpoint, 2011.

Lovins, Amory. *Reinventing Fire.* White River Junction, VT: Chelsea Green Publishing, 2014.

Lynas, Mark. *Six Degrees: Our Future on a Hotter Planet.* Washington, DC: National Geographic, 2008.

Ochoa, George, Jennifer Hoffman, and Tina Tin. *Climate: The Force That Shapes Our World and the Future of Life on Earth.* London: Rodale, 2005.

Oppenheimer, Stephen. *The Real Eve: Modern Man's Journey Out of Africa.* New York: Carroll & Graf, 2007.

Stager, Curt. *Deep Future: The Next 100,000 Years of Life on Earth.* New York: St. Martin's Press, 2011.

Walsh, Bryan, ed. *Time: Global Warming.* New York: Time, 2012.

Zalasiewicz, Jan, and Mark Williams. *The Goldilocks Planet.* Oxford: Oxford University Press, 2012.

PRIMARY SOURCES

City of New York. *Inventory of New York City Greenhouse Gas Emissions, September 2011.* Jonathan Dickinson and Andrea Tenorio. Mayor's Office of Long-Term Planning and Sustainability, New York, 2011.

Department of Defense. *Quadrennial Defense Review Report.* February 2010. www.defense.gov/qdr/images/QDR_as_of_12Feb10_1000.pdf.

Gunders, Dana. *Wasted: How America Is Losing Up to 40 Percent of Its Food from Farm to Fork to Landfill.* Natural Resources Defense Council. August 2012. www.nrdc.org/food/files/wasted-food-ip.pdf.

Intergovernmental Panel on Climate Change. "Summary for Policymakers." In *Climate Change 2007: Impacts, Adaptation and Vulnerability,* edited by M. L. Parry, O. F. Canziani, J. P. Palutikof, P. J. van der Linden, and C. E. Hanson, 7–22. Contribution of Working Group II to the Fourth Assessment Report of the Intergovernmental Panel on Climate Change. Cambridge and New York: Cambridge University Press, 2007.

Intergovernmental Panel on Climate Change. "Summary for Policymakers." In *Climate Change 2007: Mitigation,* edited by B. Metz, O. R. Davidson, P. R. Bosch, R. Dave, and L. A. Meyer, 10–23. Contribution of Working Group III to the Fourth Assessment Report of the Intergovernmental Panel on Climate Change. Cambridge and New York: Cambridge University Press, 2007.

Intergovernmental Panel on Climate Change. "Summary for Policymakers." In *Climate Change 2007: The Physical Science Basis,* edited by S. Solomon, D. Qin, M. Manning, Z. Chen, M. Marquis, K. B. Averyt, M. Tignor, and H. L. Miller, 11–18. Contribution of Working Group I to the Fourth Assessment Report of the Intergovernmental Panel on Climate Change. Cambridge and New York: Cambridge University Press, 2007.

Intergovernmental Panel on Climate Change. "Summary for Policymakers." In *Climate Change 2013: The Physical Science Basis,* edited by T. F. Stocker, D. Qin, G.-K. Plattner, M. Tignor, S. K. Allen, J. Boschung, A. Nauels, Y. Xia, V. Bex, and P. M. Midgley, 1–27. Contribution of Working Group I to the Fifth Assessment Report of the Intergovernmental Panel on Climate Change. Cambridge and New York: Cambridge University Press, 2013.

Intergovernmental Panel on Climate Change. "Summary for Policymakers." In *Managing the Risks of Extreme Events and Disasters to Advance Climate Change Adaptation,* edited by C. B. Field, V. Barros, T. F. Stocker, D. Qin, D. J. Dokken, K. L. Ebi, M. D. Mastrandrea, K. J. Mach, G.-K. Plattner, S. K. Allen, M. Tignor, and P. M. Midgley, 1–19. Special Report of Working Groups I and II of the Intergovernmental Panel on Climate Change. Cambridge and New York: Cambridge University Press, 2012.

Ogden, Joan, and Lorraine Anderson, eds. *Sustainable Transportation Energy Pathways: A Research Summary for Decision Makers.* Davis, CA: The Regents of the University of California, Davis, 2011. steps.ucdavis.edu /files/09–06-2013-STEPS-Book-A-Research-Summary-for-Decision -Makers-Sept-2011.pdf.

U.S. Department of Transportation, Federal Highway Administration. "Household Travel in America." In *2010 Status of the Nation's Highways, Bridges, and Transit: Conditions & Performance.* 2010. www.fhwa.dot .gov/policy/2010cpr/chap1.htm.

U.S. Environmental Protection Agency. *Greenhouse Gas Emissions.* September 9, 2013. www.epa.gov/climatechange/ghgemissions.

U.S. Environmental Protection Agency. *Municipal Solid Waste Generation, Recycling, and Disposal in the United States: Facts and Figures for 2010.* 2010. www.epa.gov/wastes/nonhaz/municipal/pubs/msw_2010_rev _factsheet.pdf.

ARTICLES

Alliance to Save Energy. "PC Energy Report." 2009. www.le.com
/energycampaign/downloads/PC_EnergyReport2009-US.pdf.

Appenzeller, Tim. "The Case of the Missing Carbon." *National Geographic.*
February 2004. environment.nationalgeographic.com/environment
/global-warming/missing-carbon/#page=9.

Associated Press. "Climate-Change Death Toll Put at 300,000 a Year."
NBC News.com. May 29, 2009. www.nbcnews.com/id/30998907/#.
UyEdGfldUy5.

Australia Network News. "Philippines Typhoon a 'Warning' on Climate Change:
UN Secretary-General." November 17, 2013. www.abc.net.au
/news/2013–11–17/an-philippines-typhoon-a-27warning27-on
-climate-change3a-un-/5097282.

Barboza, Tony. "U.S. Carbon Emissions Rose 2% in 2013 After Years of
Decline." *Los Angeles Times.* January 13, 2014. www.latimes.com
/science/sciencenow/la-sci-sn-carbon-emissions-rise-coal-natural
-gas-20140113,0,43142.story#axzz2s0QRNZpu.

Barclay, Eliza. "Climate Change Spurring Dengue Rise, Experts Say." *National
Geographic News.* September 21, 2007. news.nationalgeographic.com
/news/2007/09/070921-dengue-warming.html.

BBC News. "Brazil Says Amazon Deforestation Rose 28% in a Year." November
15, 2013. www.bbc.com/news/world-latin-america-24950487.

Biello, David. "Grass Makes Better Ethanol Than Corn Does." *Scientific
American.* January 8, 2008. www.scientificamerican.com/article/grass
-makes-better-ethanol-than-corn.

Black, Richard. "Fukushima's Disease Risk: A Major Fallout?" *BBC News.* July
17, 2012. www.bbc.com/news/science-environment-18870315.

Bogo, Jennifer. "Cows to Kilowatts: U.S. Farms Save Big Turning Manure to

Energy." *Popular Mechanics.* February 1, 2009. www.popularmechanics
.com/science/environment/waste/4285577.

Bond, T. C., S. J. Doherty, D. W. Fahey, P. M. Forster, T. Bernsten, B. J. De
Angelo, M. G. Flanner, et al. "Bounding the Role of Back Carbon in
the Climate System: A Scientific Assessment." *Journal of Geophysical
Research: Atmospheres* 118, no. 11 (2013): 5380–552.

Center for Sustainable Systems University of Michigan. "U.S. Environmental
Footprint." css.snre.umich.edu/css_doc/CSS08–08.pdf.

Chen, Zhu, Jin-Nan Wang, Guo-Xia Ma, Yan-Shen Zhang. "China Tackles the
Health Effects of Air Pollution." *Lancet* 382, no. 9909 (2013): 1959–60.

Cook, John, Dana Nuccitelli, Sarah A. Green, Mark Richardson, Bärbel
Winkler, Rob Painting, Robert Way, Peter Jacobs, and Andrew Skuce.
"Quantifying the Consensus on Anthropogenic Global Warming in the
Scientific Literature." *Environmental Research Letters* 8 (2013).

Corell, Robert W. "Global Climate Change and Water Resources Keynote."
2012 Annual Meeting of the Washington State Academy of Sciences.
September 20, 2012. www.washacad.org/about/files/symposiumfiles
_web/2012symposium_review_clr.pdf.

Davies, Ella. "Dinosaur Gases 'Warmed the Earth.'" *BBC Nature.* May 7, 2012.
www.bbc.co.uk/nature/17953792.

Diamond, Jared. "What's Your Consumption Factor?" *New York Times.*
January 2, 2008. www.nytimes.com/2008/01/02/opinion/02diamond
.html?pagewanted=all&_r=0.

Dickinson, Elizabeth. "Who Killed the Climate Bill?" *Foreign Policy.* July 23,
2010. www.foreignpolicy.com/articles/2010/07/23/who_killed_the
_climate_bill.

Doniger, David. "United States Records Carbon Reduction Target Under
Copenhagen Accord." *Switchboard: Natural Resources Defense Council
Staff Blog.* February 2, 2010. switchboard.nrdc.org/blogs/ddoniger
/united_states_records_carbon_r.html.

Eaton, Sam. "Carbon-Neutral Lunch: Costa Rica Looks to Lead on Climate-Friendly Ag." PRI. June 20, 2013. www.pri.org/stories/2013-06-20/carbon-neutral-lunch-costa-rica-looks-lead-climate-friendly-ag.

Economist. "The New Black." January 19, 2013. www.economist.com/news/science-and-technology/21569686-soot-even-worse-climate-was-previously-thought-new-black.

Energy Star. "Energy Star LED Bulb Challenge." www.energystar.gov/certified-products/detail/light_bulbs.

———. "What About Clothes Dryers?" www.energystar.gov/index.cfm?c=clotheswash.pr_clothes_dryers%20.

EPA. "President's Environmental Youth Award (PEYA) Winners." 2012. www2.epa.gov/education/presidents-environmental-youth-award-peya-winners.

Etheridge, D. M., L. P. Steele, R. J. Francy, and L. Lagentelds. "Atmospheric Methane Between 1000 A.D. and Present. Evidence of Anthropogenic Emissions and Climate Variability." *Journal of Geophysical Research* 103, no. 15 (1998): 979–93.

Federal Aviation Administration. "FAA Forecast Predicts Air Travel to Double in Two Decades." February 15, 2011. www.faa.gov/news/press_releases/news_story.cfm?newsId12439.

Finamore, Barbara. "China Records Its Climate Actions by Copenhagen Accord Deadline." *Switchboard: Natural Resources Defense Council Staff Blog.* February 1, 2010. switchboard.nrdc.org/blogs/bfinamore/china_records_its_climate_acti.html.

Galuszka, Peter. "With China and India Ravenous for Energy, Coal's Future Seems Assured." *New York Times.* November 12, 2012. www.nytimes.com/2012/11/13/business/energy-environment/china-leads-the-way-as-demand-for-coal-surges-worldwide.html?pagewanted=1&_r=1&.

Gettleman, Jeffrey. "Misery Follows as Somalis Try to Flee Hunger." *New York Times.* July 15, 2011. www.nytimes.com/2011/07/16/world/africa

/16somalia.html?pagewanted=all&_r=2&&version=meter+at+7&
region=FixedCenter&pgtype=Article&priority=true&module
=RegiWall-Regi&action=click.

Githeko, Andrew, Steve Lindsay, Ulisses Confalonieri, and Jonathan Patz.
"Climate Change and Vector-Borne Diseases: A Regional Analysis."
Bulletin of the World Health Organization 78, no. 9 (2000): 1136-47.
www.who.int/bulletin/archives/78(9)1136.pdf.

Gleick, Peter, and Matthew Heberger. "Devastating Drought Seems Inevitable
in American West." *Scientific American.* January 5, 2011. www
.scientificamerican.com/article/the-coming-mega-drought.

Goldenberg, Suzanne. "Just 90 Companies Caused Two-Thirds of Man-Made
Global Warming Emissions." *Guardian.* November 20, 2013. www
.theguardian.com/environment/2013/nov/20/90-companies-man
-made-global-warming-emissions-climate-change.

Gordon, Stephen, N. Bruce, J. Grigg, P. Hibberd, D. Kurmi, K. H. Lam, K.
Mortimer, et al. "Respiratory Risks from Household Air Pollution
in Low and Middle Income Countries." *Lancet Respiratory Medicine.*
September 3, 2014. www.thelancet.com/journals/lanres/article/
PIIS2213-2600(14)70168-7/fulltext.

Guardian. "Which Industries and Activities Emit the Most Carbon?" April 28,
2011. www.theguardian.com/environment/2011/apr/28/industries
-sectors-carbon-emissions.

Handwork, Brian. "Whatever Happened to the Ozone Hole?" *National
Geographic Daily News.* May 5, 2010. news.nationalgeographic.com
/news/2010/05/100505-science-environment-ozone-hole-25-years.

Hansen, James. "Can We Defuse the Global Warming Time Bomb?" *Natural
Science.* August 1, 2003. naturalscience.com/ns/articles/01–16/ns_jeh6
.html.

Hansen, Kathryn. "Water Vapor Confirmed as Major Player in Climate

Change." NASA. November 17, 2008. www.nasa.gov/topics/earth/features/vapor_warming.html.

Hinrichsen, Don. "The Oceans Are Coming Ashore." Worldwatch Institute. www.worldwatch.org/node/492.

Holland, Jennifer. "Small Wonders: The Secret Life of Marine Microfauna." *National Geographic*. November 2007. ngm.nationalgeographic.com/2007/11/marine-miniatures/holland-text.

International Energy Agency. "FAQs: Oil." www.iea.org/aboutus/faqs/oil.

Jardine, Phil. "Patterns in Palaeontology: The Paleocene–Eocene Thermal Maximum." *Patterns in Paleontology*. January 10, 2011. www.palaeontologyonline.com/articles/2011/the-paleocene-eocene-thermal-maximum.

Judkis, Maura. "Simple Green Step: Shut Down Your Computer Every Night." *U.S. News & World Report*. March 25, 2009. money.usnews.com/money/blogs/fresh-greens/2009/03/25/simple-green-step-shut-down-your-computer-every-night.

Kunzig, Robert. "The Canadian Oil Boom." *National Geographic*. March 2009. ngm.nationalgeographic.com/2009/03/canadian-oil-sands/kunzig-text/1.

———. "World Without Ice." *National Geographic*. October 2011. ngm.nationalgeographic.com/2011/10/hothouse-earth/kunzig-text/1.

LeBeau, Philip. "Whoa! 1.7 Billion Cars on the Road by 2035." *CNBC*. November 12, 2012. www.cnbc.com/id/49796736.

Lindsey, Rebecca. "Causes of Deforestation: Direct Causes." NASA. March 30, 2007. earthobservatory.nasa.gov/Features/Deforestation/deforestation_update3.php.

Loomis, Brandon. "Wildfire Season Getting Longer." *Arizona Republic*. July 22, 2013. www.azcentral.com/news/politics/articles/20130719wildfire-season-getting-longer.html.

Lovett, Rick. "Melting Glaciers Mean Double Trouble for Water Supplies." *National Geographic News*. December 20, 2011. news.nationalgeograp. hic.com/news/2011/12/1112-melting-glaciers-mean-double-trouble -for-water-supplies.

Markowitz, Ezra M., and Azim F. Shariff. "Climate Change and Moral Judgement." *Nature Climate Change* 2 (2012): 243–47.

Massey, Nathanael, and Climate Wire. "Computer Model Predicts Fewer Than 200 Deaths from Fukushima Radiation." *Scientific American*. July 17, 2012. www.scientificamerican.com/article/computer-model-predicts -fewer-than-200-deaths-fukushima-radiation.

Mayer, Lindsay Renick. "Big Oil, Big Influence." *PBS Now*. August 1, 2008. www.pbs.org/now/shows/347/oil-politics.html.

McDermott, Tricia. "Global Warming Imperils Alaska Village." *CBS Evening News*. August 22, 2006. www.cbsnews.com/news/global-warming -imperils-alaska-village.

McGarrity, John. "Analysis: EU Coal Demand Starting Decades-Long Slide." Reuters. August 30, 2013. www.reuters.com/article/2013/08/30/us- coal-demand-europe-analysis-idUSBRE97T0K120130830.

McKenna, Phil. "Former Navy SEAL Powers the Battlefield with Hybrid Generators." *Wired*. April 27, 2012. www.wired.com /dangerroom/2012/04/st_alpha_seal.

Michigan.gov. "Seatbelt History in the U.S. and Michigan." www.michigan .gov/documents/msp/Seat_belt_timeline_03_web_386202_7.pdf.

Morello, Lauren. "Phytoplankton Population Drops 40 Percent Since 1950." *Scientific American*. July 29, 2010. www.scientificamerican.com/article /phytoplankton-population.

Mott, Nicholas. "Why the Maya Fell: Climate Change, Conflict — And a Trip to the Beach?" *National Geographic News*. November 9, 2012. news .nationalgeographic.com/news/2012/11/121109-maya-civilization -climate-change-belize-science.

National Geographic. "Geothermal Energy." environment.nationalgeographic
.com/environment/global-warming/geothermal-profile.

National Weather Service. "Kansas City and Surrounding Area: Snow
Climatology." www.crh.noaa.gov/eax/?n=kcwinterstats.

Natural Resources Defense Council. "From Copenhagen Accord to Climate
Action: Tracking National Commitments to Curb Global Warming."
www.nrdc.org/international/copenhagenaccords.

———. "Renewable Energy: Wind Energy for America." www.nrdc.org/energy/
renewables/wind.asp.

National Snow & Ice Data Center. "Wildlife: Seals." nsidc.org/cryosphere
/seaice/environment/mammals_seals.html.

Open Congress. "Sen. James Inhofe." www.opencongress.org/people/money
/300055_James_Inhofe.

Owen, David. "Greenest Place in the U.S.? It's Not Where You Think." *Yale
Environment360.* October 26, 2009. e360.yale.edu/feature/greenest
_place_in_the_us_its_not_where_you_think/2203.

Paramaguru, Kharunya. "The Battle over Global Warming Is All in Your
Head." *Time.* August 19, 2013. science.time.com/2013/08/19
/in-denial-about-the-climate-the-psychological-battle-over-global
-warming/#ixzz2vDgObvnA.

Perry, Mark. "Chart of the Day: Rising Household Vehicle Ownership over
Time Belies the 'Middle Class Stagnation' Narrative." *AEIdeas.*
September 24, 2013. www.aei-ideas.org/2013/09/chart-of-the-day
-rising-household-vehicle-ownership-over-time-belies-middle
-class-stagnation.

Peterson, Erica. "EPA Carbon Limits on New Power Plants Expected
Tomorrow." NPR. January 7, 2014. wfpl.org/post/epa-carbon
-limits-new-power-plants-expected-tomorrow.

PG&E. "What Is the Smart Grid?" www.pge.com/safety/systemworks/electric
/smartgrid.

Poore, Richard Z., Richard S. Williams Jr., and Christopher Tracey. "Sea Level
and Climate." Fact Sheet #002-00. U.S. Geological Survey 2000; rev.
2011. pubs.usgs.gov/fs/fs2-00.

Popular Science. "Grease Lighting." June 2009. www.vegawatt.com/pdf
/PopularScience_5–15-09.pdf.

Ramez, Naam. "The Evidence on GMO Safety." April 28, 2013. RamezNaam
.com.

Rogers, Simon. "World Carbon Emissions: The League Table of Every
Country." *Guardian.* June 21, 2012. www.theguardian.com/environment
/datablog/2012/jun/21/world-carbon-emissions-league-table-country.

Rogers, Stephanie. "Hard Economic Times Be Damned: 10 U.S. Cities Make
Their Own Green." *Ecosalon.* October 26, 2011. ecosalon.com
/americas-greenest-cities-319.

Rosenthal, Elisabeth. "Where Did Global Warming Go?" *New York Times.*
October 15, 2011. www.nytimes.com/2011/10/16/sunday-review
/whatever-happened-to-global-warming.html?pagewanted=1&_
r=4&emc=eta1.

Rutgers Today. "Sandy's Legacy: Climate Change Is Real for New Jerseyans,
Rutgers-Eagleton Poll Finds." April 29, 2013. news.rutgers.edu
/news-releases/2013/april-2013/sandy2019s-legacy-cl-20130429
#.Uxjk6fldUy5.

Ruppel, Carol D. "Methane Hydrates and Contemporary Climate Change."
Nature Education Knowledge 3, no. 10 (2001): 29. www.nature.com
/scitable/knowledge/library/methane-hydrates-and-contemporary
-climate-change-24314790.

Sanders, Robert. "Solar Energy Could Supply One-Third of Power in U.S.
West." University of California, Berkeley. August 1, 2013. newscenter.

berkeley.edu/2013/08/01/solar-energy-could-supply-one-third-of-power-in-u-s-west.

Schmidt, Jake. "Copenhagen Accord = Climate Action—Update." *Switchboard: Natural Resources Defense Council Staff Blog.* February 1, 2010. switchboard.nrdc.org/blogs/jschmidt/copenhagen_accord_climate _action.html.

Seager, R., M. F. Ting, I. Held, V. Kushnir, J. Lu, G. Vecchi, H. P. Huang, et al. "Model Projections of an Imminent Transition to a More Arid Climate in Southwestern North America." *Science* 316, no. 5828 (2007): 1181–84.

Silver, Jonathan. "Nature Adapts to Survive Climate Change." *Reuters: The Great Debate.* March 15, 2013. blogs.reuters.com/great-debate/2013/03/15 /nature-adapts-to-survive-climate-change.

Stranger, Clay. "China Smog: Can Energy Efficiency Stop 'Airmageddon'?" *Christian Science Monitor.* November 10, 2013. www.csmonitor.com /Environment/Energy-Voices/2013/1110/China-smog-Can-energy-efficiency-stop-airmageddon.

SustainableBusiness.com. "India Announces World's Largest Solar Plant by Far." September 30, 2013. www.sustainablebusiness.com/index.cfm/go/news .display/id/25246.

The Official Site of the Empire State Building. "Sustainability & Efficiency." www.esbnyc.com/sustainability_energy_efficiency.asp.

Tollefson, Jeff. "The 8,000-Year-Old Climate Puzzle." *Nature.* March 25, 2011. www.nature.com/news/2011/110325/full/news.2011.184.html.

Union of Concerned Scientists. "Global Warming Skeptic Organizations." www .ucsusa.org/global_warming/solutions/fight-misinformation/global -warming-skeptic.html.

United Nations News Centre. "UN: 2010 Among Deadliest Years for Disasters, Urges Better Preparedness." January 24, 2011. www.un.org/apps /news/story.asp?NewsID=37357#.UyEf8PldUy5.

U.S. Department of Energy. "Myths About Energy in Schools." www.nrel.gov /docs/fy02osti/31607.pdf.

———. "Rebuilding It Better: Greensburg, Kansas." www 1.eere.energy.gov/office_eere/pdfs/49315.pdf.

U.S. Energy Information Administration. "Household Heating Fuels Vary Across the Country." www.eia.gov/todayinenergy/detail.cfm?id=3690.

U.S. Geological Survey. "Hydroelectric Power Water Use." water.usgs.gov/edu /wuhy.html.

University of British Columbia Faculty of Law. "Climate Change Litigation: Inuit v. the U.S. Electricity Generation Industry." April 24, 2009. www .law.ubc.ca/files/pdf/enlaw/climatechange_04_24_09.pdf.

Wagstaff, Keith. "China's Massive Pollution Problem." *Week*. November 9, 2013. theweek.com/article/index/252440/chinas-massive-pollution-problem.

Walsh, Bryan. "Cap and Trade Is Dead (Really, Truly, I'm Not Kidding). Who's to Blame?" *Time*. July 22, 2010. science.time.com/2010/07/22/cap-and -trade-is-dead-really-truly-im-not-kidding-whos-to-blame.

Weart, Spencer. "The Discovery of Global Warming." The American Institute of Physics. February 2014. www.aip.org/history/climate/co2.htm#S2.

Weber, Christopher L., and H. Scott Matthews. "Food Miles and the Relative Climate Impacts of Food Choices in the United States." *Environmental Science & Technology* 42, no. 10 (2008): 3508–13.

Wilkinson, David, Euan Nisbet, and Graeme Ruxton. "Could Methane Produced by Sauropod Dinosaurs Have Helped Drive Mesozoic Climate Warmth?" *Current Biology* 22, no. 9 (2012): R292–93.

Windridge, Melanie. "Fear of Nuclear Power Is Out of All Proportion to the Actual Risks." *Guardian*. April 4, 2011. www.guardian.co.uk/science /blog/2011/apr/04/fear-nuclear-power-fukushima-risks.

Wong, Edward. "Air Pollution Linked to 1.2 Million Premature Deaths in China." *New York Times*. April 1, 2013. www.nytimes.com/2013/04/02

/world/asia/air-pollution-linked-to-1–2-million-deaths-in-china
.html?_r=1&.

World Bank. "CO_2 Emissions (Metric Tons per Capita)." 2014. data
.worldbank.org/indicator/EN.ATM.CO2E.PC.

World Nuclear Association. "Nuclear Power in the USA." September 2014.
www.world-nuclear.org/info/country-profiles/countries-T-Z/USA
-nuclear-power.

Worldwatch Institute. "U.S. Public Still Unconvinced on Climate Change."
www.worldwatch.org/node/6300.

PHOTO CREDITS

Ingram Publishing/Alamy: 60 (bottom)

iStockphoto: 86 (bottom), 87 (top)

James Jordan Photography/Flickr/Getty Images: 115

Juanmonino/Getty Images/iStockphoto: 120–21

Elena Kalistratova/Vetta/Getty Images: 35

Mark Karrass/Corbis: 80–81

Erik Kolstad/iStockphoto: 42

Ozan Köse/Istock: 89

Scott Latham/Fotolia: 191

James Laurie/Shutterstock: 25

Winston Lue/Fotolia: 114

Eirini_Manousaki/iStockphoto.com: 176

Marek Mnich/Getty Images/iStockphoto: 101

NASA: 3, 30, 76

NASA, courtesy of the Lunar and Planetary Institute: 136–37, 145

NASA, ESA, T. Megeath (University of Toledo) and M. Robberto (STScI): 31

NASA-GISS, CDIAC, NOAA, ESRL: 5

NASA Goddard's Scientific Visualization Studio: 2

Nancy Nehring/iStockphoto: 82

one AND only/Shutterstock: 188–89

Photodisc/Getty Images: 6–7, 14, 66, 69, 124, 138

Dmitry Pichugin/Fotolio: 54–55, 89

Radius Images/Corbis: 118

Ruppel/USGS: 133

Peter Ryle/Alamy: 129

Marcus Schieder/iStockphoto: 47

Scripps Institution of Oceanography/NOAA Earth System Research Laboratory: 71

JANA SHEA/iStockphoto: 87 (bottom)

SHIGEMITSU/iStockphoto: 113

INDEX

Page numbers in **bold** refer to photos or charts and their captions.

Agassiz, Louis, 43
agriculture
    "be the change" strategies, 100
    development of, 52–53
    in drought conditions, 128–30, **129**
    genetically modified crops, 117, 120–21
    greenhouse gas emissions from, 52–53, 116–17
    small-farm initiatives, 164, 167
Amazon rainforest, 19–22, **22**, 26
Antarctica
    ice sheet, 72, 81–83, 127
    warming trend, 77, **78**
anthropogenic climate change
    carbon dioxide levels before and since Industrial Revolution,
        5–6, **44**, 58–59, **59**, 96–97
    versus natural processes in climate change, 35–36, 41
    politically polarized beliefs about, 139, 149–50, 151
    possible impact of Agricultural Revolution, 52–53
    reliance on fossil fuels, 56–57
    scientific study and consensus on, 5–6, 66–72, 95–99, **96**,
        101
    use of wood as fuel, 56
Arctic region
    greenhouse gas release from melting permafrost, 77–78,
        133–34
    Greenland ice sheet, 43, 72, 81–82, 127, 136–37
    rapid warming in, **2**, 77
    sea ice loss, 78–80, **79**, 82, **91**, 92
    vulnerability to ice melt, 82–83
    wildlife, **91**, 92

Arrhenius, Svante, 66–68
automobiles. *See* transportation

Bangladesh, 126, **126**
Ban Ki-moon, 85–88
"be the change" strategies. *See also* measures to combat climate
   change
   assessing energy usage, 18
   impact of small changes, 8–9
   reducing agricultural emissions, 100
   reducing fuel emissions, 63, 73, 94
   reducing household emissions, 27, 45, 53, 184
   reducing industry emissions, 119, 135, 147, 185
   reducing waste emissions, 154–55, 169
   sharing information and tips, 195
biofuels, 157, 158, 179–80, **180**, 193–94
black carbon, 104–5
Bloomberg, Mike, 160–61
Brazil, 116, 152, 167, 180

"Can We Defuse the Global Warming Time Bomb?" (Hansen),
   136–37
carbon, black, 104
carbon dioxide
   absorption by plants, 16, **16**, 43
   "be the change" strategy, 18
   from burning of fossil fuels, 15–17, 41, 68–69, **69**, 101, **110**
   carbon cycle feedback, 133
   consequences of future rise in emissions, 125–34, **126**, **129**,
      131, **132**, **133**
   correlation with temperature and climate, 66–72, **67**
   in evolution of complex life on Earth, 35–36
   ice age levels, 35, **35**, 43, 48–49, 66–67, 72
   in ice and permafrost, 72, 77–78, 95–96, 133
   levels before and since Industrial Revolution, 5–6, **44**, 58–59,
      59, 96–97
   measurement records, 70, **71**, 168

ocean acidification, 24, 92–94
ocean storage and emission of, 23–24, 50, 68–70
in Permian-Triassic extinction, 38–39, 41
persistence in atmosphere, 57, 58, 68–69, **69**
as predominant greenhouse gas, 101–2, **102, 103**
recent decline in emissions, 109, **110**
carbon intensity standards, 162–63
cars. *See* transportation
Charney, Jule, 70–71
China, 106, 109–11, **112**, 140, 166, 168
Clean Air Act, 109, 156–57, **157**
clean energy sources. *See* renewable and clean energy sources
climate
    factors in, 19–26, **20, 21, 22**
    versus weather, 19
climate change. *See also* anthropogenic climate change; "be the
        change" strategies; measures to combat climate change
    current consequences of, 3–4, 75–76
    throughout Earth's history, 34–37, **35,** 39–44, **40, 42**
    feedback phenomenon, 34
    future scenarios, 125–34, **126, 129, 131, 132, 133**
    glacier melt, **1,** 4, 47–50, **48, 49,** 81–83, **82,** 130, **131**
    glossary of terms, 196–200
    impact on wildlife, **91,** 91–92
    lawsuits concerning, 80
    mass extinction and, 37–39
    public indifference toward, 138–41, 151–52, 154
    refugees from drought, **89,** 89–90
    refugees from flooding, 1, 3–4, 83–84, 125–27, **126,** 134
    resources for further information, 201
    sea ice melt, 78–80, **79,** 82, **91,** 92
    temperature trends and seasonal variations, 74–75, **75, 76**
    use of climate models, 70–71, 124–25
"Climate Change and Moral Judgment" (Markowitz and
        Shariff), 139–40
coal
    creation of, 15–17

coal (*continued*)
    for electricity generation, **60**, 108–11
    large-scale use during Industrial Revolution, **57**, 57–59, **59**
    usage in China, 109–11, **112**
combatting global warming. *See* "be the change" strategies;
    measures to combat climate change
composting, 154–55, 181–82
Cooke, John, 98
Copenhagen Accord, 152–53, 165–66, 167, 168, 178
coral reef bleaching, 93
Costa Rica, 167–68

deforestation
    emission of greenhouse gases, 16–17, 26, 56, 116
    forest conservation programs, 107, 119
disease, 88–89, 104–5
droughts and wildfires
    displacement of populations, **89**, 89–90
    Dust Bowl, 130
    predictions on, 127–30, **129**
    with rising temperatures, **89**, 89–91, **90**, **129**
    Sudan genocide and, 128
    throughout Earth's history, 50, 54

Earth. *See also* ice age
    climate fluctuations, 34–37, **35**, 39–44, **40**, **42**
    emergence of life, **32**, 32–36
    formation of, 30–32, **31**
    greenhouse effect, 12–15, **15**
    mass extinction, 37–39
    perfect climate for human life, 2–3, **3**, 11
electricity. *See also* renewable and clean energy sources
    average daily usage by individuals, 172
    coal-generated power, **60**, 108–11
    consumption by turned-off appliances, 184
    home energy usage, **173**, 173–75
    as leading greenhouse gas emitter, **106**, 107

from recycled waste, 163–64, 192–93
state clean energy laws on, 162
European Union, 105, 109, **117**, 148, 167, 181

farming. *See* agriculture
flooding
    of coastal cities, 3–4
    during Earth's interglacial periods, 51–52
    with increasingly frequent and intense storms, 85–88, **86**, **87**,
        127
    from melting sea ice, 78–80, **79**
    of Pacific islands, 1, **1**, **84**
    refugees from, 1, 3–4, 83–84, 125–27, **126**, 134
    with sea level rise, **1**, 125–27, **126**
    from storm surges, 79–80, **86**
fluorinated gases (F-gases), 103–4
food waste, 154–55, 169, 181–82
forestry
    conservation programs, 107, 119
    greenhouse gas emissions from deforestation, 16–17, 26, 56,
        116
fossil fuels
    carbon dioxide emissions from, 15–17, 41, 68–69, **69**, 101,
        110
    coal, **57**, 57–59, **59**, **60**, 108–11, **112**
    creation of, 15–17
    human reliance upon, 56, 62, 118
    natural gas, 108–9, **110**
    new sources of, 80, 108–9, **114**, 114–15
    oil, 59–61, **61**, 112–15, **113**, **114**
fuel efficiency standards, 61–62, 113, 157–58, 177–78

genetically modified organisms (GMOs), 117, 120–21
geothermal energy, 186–87, **187**
glaciers
    calving, **82**
    deposit of sediment and creation of fertile land, **42**, 52, 129

glaciers (*continued*)
  Greenland and Antarctic ice sheets, 43, 72, 81–82, 127,
      136–37
  during ice age, 4, 47–52, **48, 49**, 50, 55
  sea level rise from glacial meltwater, **2**, 81–83, 131
  water shortages from shrinkage of glaciers, 4, 81, 130, **131**
global warming. *See* anthropogenic climate change; climate
      change
glossary of terms, 196–200
GMOs, 117, 120–21
Great Dying (Permian-Triassic extinction), 37–39, 41
greenhouse effect, 12–15, **13, 15**
greenhouse gas emissions. *See also* carbon dioxide; methane
  from agriculture, 52–53, 116–17
  components of, 101–4, **102, 103**
  Copenhagen Accord goals, 152–53, 165–66, 167, 168, 178
  correlation with climate change, 43–44, 66–68
  from deforestation, 16–17, 26, 56, 116
  by developing nations, 76, 118, 149, 152, 167
  from energy production, **106**, 108–11, **110, 112**
  from industry, **57**, 57–59, **59**, 110–11, **112**, 115
  Kyoto Protocol goals, 148–49, 159, 167
  leading producers of, **105**, 105–8, **106, 107**
  limiting through Clean Air Act, 109, 156–57, **157**
  from transportation, 62, **106**, 112–15, **113**
Greenland ice sheet, 43, 72, 81–82, 127, 136–37
Guzman, Andrew, 128

Hansen, James, 70, 136–37
heat waves and tropical diseases, 88–89
Högbom, Arvid, 67–68
hominins, 46–47, **47**, 50–52
human-caused climate change. *See* anthropogenic climate
      change
hydroelectric power, 190–91, **191**

ice age
  greenhouse gas levels during, 35, **35**, 43, 48–49, 66–67, 72
  hominin survival of, 46–47, **47**, 50–52
  interglacial periods, 48–49, 50, 51, 137
  last glacial maximum, 51–52
  Little Ice Age, 55
  Milankovitch cycles and positive feedback, 46–50
  Snowball Earth, 34–36
  temperature during, 4
ice loss. *See* Arctic region; glaciers
India, 105, 113, **113**, 152, 166–67, 190
Industrial Revolution
  carbon dioxide levels before and since, 5–6, **44**, 58–59, **59**,
    96–97
  large-scale use of coal, **57**, 57–59, **59**
industry
  "be the change" strategies, 119, 135, 147, 185
  companies emitting most greenhouse gases, **107**, 107–8
  as source of greenhouse gas emissions, **57**, 57–59, **59**, 110–
    11, **112**, 115
Intergovernmental Panel on Climate Change (IPCC)
  creation and purpose of, 72
  on current consequences of climate change, 75, 88, 97
  on existence of anthropogenic climate change, 72, 97
  on land area under drought conditions, 89
  on loss of glacier ice, 81
  predictions based upon climate data and models, 125, 127,
    131
  on recent rise in global temperature, 74
  recommendations on greenhouse gas levels, 6
  on rise in sea level, 83

Keeling, Charles David, 70
Kiribati, 1, **1**, 3–4
Kyoto Protocol, 148–49, 159, 167

Lynas, Mark, 126

Manabe, Syukuro, 70
Markowitz, Ezra, 139–40
measures to combat climate change. *See also* "be the change"
    strategies
    alternative-fuel vehicles, 157–58, 175, 178–81, **179**, **180**
    by businesses, 163–64, 174–75
    by city governments, 159–61, **160**
    Copenhagen Accord, 152–53, 165–66, 167, 168, 178
    by countries around world, 165–68
    creation of Intergovernmental Panel on Climate Change
        (IPCC), 72
    energy-efficient homes and buildings, 172–77, **176**
    fuel efficiency standards, 61–62, 113, 157–58, 177–78
    Kyoto Protocol, 148–49, 159, 167
    by Obama administration, 152–53, **153**, 157–58, 177–78
    recycling, 181–83, **183**
    by state governments, 161–63
    by students, 164–65, **165**
    United Nations Framework Convention on Climate
        Change, 148
    by U.S. military, 158–59
methane
    agricultural emissions, 52–53, 100, 116–17
    from dinosaurs, 39–40, **40**
    from food waste in landfills, 155, 169, 193
    as greenhouse gas, 102–3
    in oceanic and permafrost methane ice, 38, 50, 77–78, **132**,
        133, 133–34
Milankovitch cycles, 46–47
mollusks, ocean acidification and, 24, 93

natural gas, 108–9, **110**
New York City, **160**, 160–61, 163
nitrous oxide, 103
nuclear power, 191–92

Obama administration, 152–53, **153**, 157–58, 177–78
oceans
    acidification, 24, 92–94
    methane ice in, **132**, **133**, 134
    regulation of atmospheric temperature, 23
    storage and emission of carbon dioxide, 23–24, 50, 68–70
oil
    creation of, 15–17
    new sources of, 80, **114**, 114–15
    for transportation uses, 59–61, **61**, 112–13, **113**
Oppenheimer, Stephen, 50–51
Overheated (Guzman), 128

permafrost, 38, 50, 77–78, **132**, 133–34
Permian-Triassic extinction, 37–39, 41
petroleum. *See* oil
plants
    carbon dioxide absorption, 16, **16**
    contribution to precipitation, 26
    migration to cooler regions, 92
    urban trees, 161
Plass, Gilbert N., 68
polar ice
    Arctic sea ice, 78–80, **79**, 82, **91**, 92
    Greenland and Antarctic ice sheets, 43, 72, 81–82, 127,
        136–37
politics of climate change
    disagreements over cap and trade system, 153–54
    influence of oil and gas industry, 150–51
    skepticism and denial of global warming, 139–40, 149–50,
        151
    start of political polarization, 149
    viewpoint differences along party lines, 138–40, 146–47, 149,
        151, 162
population displacement
    by drought, **89**, 89–90
    by flooding, 1, 3–4, 83–84, 125–27, **126**, 134

population displacement (*continued*)
    global migration during ice age, 50–51
power generation. *See* electricity
precipitation, 24–26, **25**, 55

recycling
    composting, 154–55, 181–82
    energy from waste, 163–64, 192–93
refugees. *See* population displacement
renewable and clean energy sources
    biofuels, 157, 158, 179–80, **180**, 193–94
    geothermal steam, 186–87, **187**
    nuclear power, 191–92
    sun, **189**, 189–90
    waste recycling, 163–64, 192–93
    water, 190–91, **191**
    wind, 187–88, **188**
resources for further information, 201
Revelle, Roger, 69–70
Ruddiman, William, 52

sea ice, 78–80, **79**, 82, **91**, 92
sea level rise
    acceleration of, 83
    flooding and displacement of populations, 1, 3–4, 83–84, **84**, 125–27, **126**, 134
    from glacial meltwater, **2**, 81–83, 131
    during ice age, 137
    potential from melting polar caps, 134
    predictions on, 125–26, **126**
Sharif, Azim, 139–40
Shen Kua, 43
Six Degrees (Lynas), 126
solar energy, **189**, 189–90
storms. *See* flooding
Sudan genocide, 128
Suess, Hans, 68–69

sun
    clean energy from, **189**, 189–90
    effect on climate, 19–22, **20**, **21**, **22**

temperature
    consequences of future rise in, 125–34
    impact of small rise in, 4, 75–76
    trends over time, 74–75, **76**
    worldwide rise in, **2**
transportation
    alternative-fuel vehicles, 157–58, 175, 178–81, **179**, **180**
    "be the change" strategies, 63, 73, 94
    carbon intensity standards, 162–63
    demand for oil, 59–61, **61**, 112–15, **113**
    fuel efficiency standards, 61–62, 113, 157–58, 177–78
    as major greenhouse gas emitter, 62, **106**, 112
    state initiatives to reduce emissions, 162
tropical diseases, 88–89
Tyndall, John, 66, **67**

Venus, **13**, 13–14

waste
    "be the change" strategies, 154–55, 169
    composting, 154–55, 181–82
    electricity from, 163–64, 192–93
    methane emissions from landfill food waste, 155, 169, 193
water power, 190–91, **191**
water shortages. *See also* droughts and wildfires
    contamination of fresh groundwater, 1, 4
    from glacier shrinkage, 4, 81, 130, **131**
water vapor, 101, 104
wildfires, 89–91
wind
    clean energy from, 187–88, **188**
    effect on climate, 22–23